R Volga

RUSSIA

R Terek

CHECHNYA

Grozny

KABARDINO-
BALKARIA

INGUSHETIA

NORTH
OSSETIA

Vladikavkaz

Daryal Pass

Caucasus

Roka

Georgian Military Highway

Mountains

SOUTH
OSSETIA

Chinvali

GEORGIA

Gori

Tbilisi

R Kura

Goryelovka

ARMENIA

Gyumri

AZERBAIJAN

Abovian

Yerevan

R Kura

Shamiram

THE SPIRIT-WRESTLERS

PHILIP MARSDEN

The Spirit-Wrestlers

A RUSSIAN JOURNEY

HarperCollins*Publishers*

HarperCollins*Publishers*
77–85 Fulham Palace Road,
Hammersmith, London W6 8JB

Published by HarperCollins*Publishers* 1998
Copyright © Philip Marsden 1998

The author asserts the moral right to
be identified as the author of this work
A catalogue record for this book
is available from the British Library

ISBN 0 00 255852 1

Illustrations by Ken Lewis
Map by Leslie Robinson

Set in PostScript Linotype Minion by
Rowland Phototypesetting Ltd
Bury St Edmunds, Suffolk

Printed and bound in Great Britain by
Caledonian International Book
Manufacturing Ltd, Glasgow

For Charlotte

CONTENTS

7

GLOSSARY

aoul – Caucasian village
apparat – the Soviet bureaucracy
apparatchik – Soviet bureaucrat
ataman – a local Cossack chief, elected by his community
banya – communal steam bath
bashlyk – woollen hood, worn in the Caucasus and by Cossacks
basturma – cured ham, spiced with peppers
beryozovitsa – birch-sap wine
beshmet – Cossack tunic
blokadnik – veteran of the defence of Leningrad during the 900-day
    siege by the Nazis
bulava – ceremonial mace, ataman's symbol of office
burkha – sleeveless sheepskin cape
cherkesska – a loose-fitting tunic, adopted by Cossacks from the
    Caucasian peoples, characterised by a row of charges on each
    side of the chest
Cossacks – a military people, defined less by ethnic allegiance than
    by fiercely independent traditions, originally of the southern
    steppe
Doukhobor – 'spirit-wrestler', radical sectarian
dyedushka – colloquial form of 'grandfather'
esaul – the deputy of an ataman
giaour – (Turkish) non-Muslim, infidel
izba – a wooden cabin, traditional dwelling of Russian villages
kazak – (Arabic) freebooting soldier, root of 'Cossack'
kocak – Yezidi caste of dancers
kolbasa – salami-type sausage
kolkhoz – Soviet collective farm
kompot – a home-made cordial

9

koumiss – fermented mare's milk

kriuvka – notation system for Russian sacred music

krug – literally 'circle', a Cossack meeting

kulak – literally 'fist', a loosely-defined term for any peasant who had a degree of private property

kurgan – Scythian burial mound

kvass – traditional Russian drink, brewed from rye flour and malt

liman – delta, lagoon

Molokan – 'milk-drinker', sectarian similar in doctrine to Doukhobors, but accepts Scriptures

muzhik – Russian peasant

nagaika – ancient knout-type weapon, favoured by Cossacks

oblast – Russian region

Old Believer – schismatic from the Russian Orthodox Church

papakha – Astrakhan hat, worn by Caucasians and Cossacks

pelmeni – Russian dish of ravioli-type parcels of meat, served with sour cream

pir – member of the Yezidi priestly caste

Priguny – (literally 'jumpers') branch of the Molokans

raskol – the seventeenth schism in the Russian Church, from which stemmed the Old Believers

samizdat – illicit publishing, practised during the Soviet period

samogon – home-distilled spirit

shashka – Cossack sword

shashlik – spit-roasted meat

sheikh – member of the Yezidi princely caste, also with sacred functions

smetana – a semi-curdled cream

sobraniye – meeting, term used by both Doukhobors and Molokans

stanitsa – Cossack settlement

starets – holy man

syta – traditional Russian mead

voeveda – town governor in the tsarist period

voisko – literally 'host', Cossack regiment

volnitsa – freedom, exemplified by Cossack life

Yezidi – Kurdish follower of Sheikh Adi

zal – hall

'Look what the Bolsheviks have done to the horses!'

Russian villagers on seeing the arrival on their collective farm
of a group of Bactrian camels

PRELUDE:
A WINTER IN MOSCOW

For the best part of one post-Soviet Moscow winter I travelled in to the Lenin Library and read stories of Cossacks and Old Believers and plotted a journey to the south.

It was a long winter. Over the months it drained the colour from the city's public face – from the fur-coated bundles on the metro trains, the ranks of anonymous buildings, the milky skies. The only exception was upriver from the Lenin Library where a host of orange hard-hats swarmed over the reconstruction of the cathedral.

Of that improbable building, nothing had existed until New Year's Day when the Patriarch of Moscow and all Russia, Aleksei II, bent his patriarchal back and laid the first stone. Originally the cathedral had been built to commemorate Russia's victory over Napoleon's Grande Armée and dedicated to he whom they had most to thank: Christ the Saviour. It had been a vast building, big enough for ten thousand worshippers. But in 1931 Stalin dynamited it to make room for his Palace of the Soviets. The palace was to be thirteen hundred feet high, topped by a statue of Lenin so large that even his index finger would be nineteen feet long – until the planners realised the clay beneath would not support such a structure. An open-air swimming-pool was put there instead.

For reasons I could not fathom, the Lenin Library issued me with a reader's card usually reserved for eminent professors and high-ranking government officials. The card gave me access to Zal no. 1, where pallid scholars sat all day hunched over volumes from which they never looked up. They never noticed, therefore, the little marks of privilege that distinguished Zal no. 1 from all the other zals – the succulents and ferns on top of each desk, the bun-haired woman who watered them, or the billows of pink curtains which bordered thirty-foot-high windows. Too much of *my* time, however, was spent gazing out of those windows at the golden cupolas of the Kremlin, and out beyond them to the factory chimneys which leaked streams of grey smoke into the grey sky.

In September 1812, Napoleon Bonaparte stood at the Kremlin windows. He was gazing out at the city he had conquered. It was ablaze. Whole quarters were subsiding beneath flames which had been ignited by the Russians themselves. He saw at once that the fire was the 'herald of great disasters'.

'What extraordinary resolve!' he muttered. 'What men! These are Scythians!'

The emperor knew the passage in Book IV of Herodotus's *Histories* in which the Scythians defeat the Persians by drawing the enemy back into their own territory, then destroying everything.

But talk of Russians and Scythians put me on my guard. It filled me with the suspicion I'd reserved for glib phrases like 'Asiatic cruelty' and 'the Slavic soul'. Pitfalls for outsiders, I concluded, and steering round them, aimed for the dissenters and misfits of the Russian fringe.

There, by chance, I stumbled on a mystical movement known as Scythianism. Instigated at the time of the Revolution, it counted Aleksandr Blok among its devotees, and in his poem 'Scythians' he wrote: 'Yes, we are Scythians! Yes, we are Asiatics . . ./Russia is a sphinx, triumphant and mournful.'

Several years earlier, I had been to St Petersburg for the first time. It was mid-summer and the air was thick with flies. The city's benign grid of canals, its cliff-like façades, its by-the-yard classicism left me unmoved. Only in the collection of Scythian gold in the Hermitage was there any sense of the vigour which Peter's capital so lacked. The collection had been gathered – largely by looting Cossacks – from graves in the Ukraine and the south of Russia. At the time I had looked at it with awe, at those miraculous curled-up Scythian wolves, the running golden stags, all the fluency and ease of the animal style, and saw no relevance at all to the present. But after reading Blok, I refiled those Scythian beasts with the things about the Russian winter that were conspiring to send me south.

For five years, I'd been skirting around Russia. I'd spent long periods in Belarus, in Lithuania, in the stony uplands of Armenia. I'd ambled through Moldova, Ukraine, Georgia and Azerbaijan. I'd watched like everyone else the sudden collapse of the Soviet Union, sensing that what happened in Russia would somehow define the new century – just as it had, more than any other country on earth, defined the old. But the more time I spent here, at its centre, the more I felt drawn back to its rim, to its burning radicals, to its remoter villages and the ambiguities of its fraying southern border.

In mid-January, the temperature dropped. The black waters of the Moscow river clogged and froze. Light snow swept over the ice. In the hours before dawn a stillness fell upon the city as if the earth itself had stopped spinning. One night when it hit thirty-three below, I remember walking home and feeling the breath freezing in my throat. But most Muscovites agreed that it wasn't a cold winter.

Early February came and the Moscow river thawed. Tabletops of ice drifted through the capital, past the White House, through the loop by the Sparrow Hills and out again into the forests. On the metro the fur coats became fewer. The orange hard-hats at Christ the Saviour finished the foundations and started on the walls. Clear days shone between the grey. Looking out of the Lenin Library window one morning, I saw the entire city fish-eyed in the Kremlin's golden cupolas.

Each morning in the yard below my flat, there now appeared a woman with a broom who replaced the wintery scrape-scraping of snow shovels with an odd litany of shouting. 'May the devil take you! The devil dance on your grave! Jokers! Criminals! This isn't a country, it's a prison!'

Such was the vitriol of her cries that it occurred to me that she swept the yard not because she had to, but out of some desperate need for self-expression. When I talked to her, it turned out she was the widow of a former Soviet ambassador to Brazil.

'I am a spiritual man,' said a spiritual-looking man in the Alexandrovsky Gardens. 'Please give me some money so that I may spend the day in prayer.'

At the open-air book market I came across Boris. He had travelled up from his southern town hidden in the train's luggage compartment; the money he'd saved had gone on a three-volume edition of Borges, a book of medieval witchcraft and a cassette of Irish music. He had a high regard for the Celts and in his town had started 'secret cell of IRA'. One night he'd pulled a balaclava over his face and sprayed FREE IRELAND! on the railway bridges. The authorities didn't mind as it was in English, and no one knew where Ireland was anyway.

Nor did Darya from Borodino when she was instructed, in a dream, to study the Irish language. She and I had been on the same course the year before at the University of Galway, and when I went to see her in Russia, I reminded her of the amazement the Connemara fishermen showed at a Russian speaking fluent Irish. But she had never noticed it. She was now studying to be a nun.

16

Generations of force-fed ideology had not diminished that peculiarly Russian passion for belief. But in Moscow at least, it had certainly distorted it. Each time I went to see Christ the Saviour, and the cranes and the scaffolding and the orange hats had climbed yet higher into the heavens, I could not help feeling a strange sense of vertigo.

In late February, a newcomer appeared in Zal no. 1. He had a sage's beard and an impish face. Each afternoon he arrived at the same time, with the same chin-high stack of books, and always chose the same seat. When after a week or so I found an opportunity to talk to him, I found him much younger than I'd thought. He was called Sergei and was trying to work out when exactly we should expect the Second Coming. He was an Old Believer of the 'priestless' division.

Sergei was attached to the monastery at Preobrazhensky and, expecting him to refuse, I asked him one day if he would take me there. He looked at me askance: 'Just so long as you do not ask us any questions.'

On a moonlit evening we met in front of the library. Fresh snow squeaked beneath our boots. Sergei took from his pocket a remote key, and the electronic locks of a brand new Land Rover Discovery clunked open.

'Smart car,' I said.

'My boss's.'

'Who is your boss?'

'Bandit.'

Sergei's boss was in fact a senior executive in one of the larger oil companies, but as he was currently 'sunning his back' in Cyprus, Sergei had the use of the Land Rover. A driver by day, Sergei's real passion, indulged after hours in the recesses of the Lenin Library, was the apocalypse. One by one, as we purred round the eastern edge of the Garden Ring, he tossed aside the bastions of Russian culture: 'Books are shit ... art is shit ... the Church is shit ... all culture is crap.'

To Sergei, worldly endeavour had ceased to have any significance in 1666. That was the year in which the Old Believers, as they became known, broke away from the main Russian Church in reaction to the reforms of Patriarch Nikon. Persecuted, hunted down, many Old Believers simply gathered in their churches and burned themselves to death. Others fled to the far corners of the empire – the frozen north, Siberia, the southern steppe. From their isolation they declared Nikon to be the Antichrist, the Tsar his demonic accomplice and their own diaspora the True Church. They were the 'Fourth Rome', the last stage before the Parousia.

Sergei leaned back. One hand foraged in his beard. Since the time of Christ, he continued, the true Church had fled like a tormented virgin from one philanderer to the next – from Rome to Byzantium, chased out of Byzantium by the Turk, and thence to Moscow. The heretical reforms of Patriarch Nikon had proved Moscow to be as corrupt as all the others, and only the Old Believers, scattered in the wilderness and waiting for the Second Coming, could claim to be the true protectors of the Church's honour.

Catherine the Great, whose self-professed holiness enabled her to make even the date of her smallpox inoculation an annual day of obligation, had a soft spot for the Old Believers. Under her reign they re-established a community in Moscow and showed themselves diligent in business and selfless during an epidemic of bubonic plague. The empress rewarded them with a piece of land and on this they built the Preobrazhensky monastery.

Sergei swung the Land Rover off the main road and into a dimly-lit courtyard. Light snow had begun to fall. In the middle of the yard was a small church, surrounded by frosted trees. The service had already begun. The elders were reading their readings and the old women kissed the icons at regular intervals. It was very cold and very dark. The service went on for three hours.

Afterwards I went with Sergei into a back room. A brazier stood in the middle and its flames sent flickering shadows into the room's low vault. Some of the elders leaned forward to warm their hands, others sat gazing at the flames. The light played on the Old Testament faces and as we talked and the talk mellowed and even Sergei appeared content, I looked at each one of those wilderness men – with their rigid convictions, their hirsute and timeless faces – and was left with the impression not so much of a doom-soaked sect as one passionately committed to survival.

The books of the Lenin Library had yielded a fair crop of minor sects and dissenters – groups like the Judaisers (hounded for their rational thought), the Sheared (drowned by the authorities), the Castrated (exiled), the Wanderers, the Jumpers, the Icon-Wrestlers. But as to their continued existence, a weary professor of history was sceptical: 'That was in the old days. Stalin got rid of the last ones.'

Then one evening in mid-March I met a doctor who said that among his patients he had a member of the Doukhobor sect. I had read a little about the Doukhobors. Their name means literally 'spirit-wrestler', and the tsarist authorities had sent them on an odyssey of exile around the old empire. In the end they'd emigrated to Canada, where they still speak a Russian frozen in the nineteenth century. But there'd been no indication that any remained in Russia.

I telephoned the Doukhobor and arranged to meet him at the metro station. I spotted him at once – stocky and broad-faced, and quite still among the flowing Moscow crowds. We went to my flat and talked about Tolstoy, who had taken the Doukhobors to heart and helped them leave Russia. I asked him how many remained in Russia and he said: 'A great number near Tula and also in the south.'

When I showed him a map he prodded a finger at a whole series of steppe villages near Rostov. 'But I am not from there,' he said.

He looked more closely at the map, mouthing the place names as he read them. His finger ran south across the steppe, over the Caucasus to a point in the far south of Georgia where the old Russian empire bordered with Turkey.

'Here. I was born here,' he said, tapping the map. 'On the edge of the world.'

For three days in mid-April the snow returned. In the morning the puddles were crusted with ice and it seemed to me that warmth would never again return to that heavy-hearted city. The ambassador's widow leaned on her broom and scowled at the late snow: 'Nowadays the weather and the nature are no longer married.'

But then a strange thing happened. Within a single day the buds burst open and the bare-branch skylines became tinged with green. There was no spring as such. The Moscow river rose two feet and grew swifter. One afternoon I returned from the Lenin Library by the usual route and a man stepped onto the metro in shirt-sleeves. He wiped his forehead and in that single gesture convinced me that it was time to leave Moscow – less because he'd brought the heat of summer into the carriage than that I recognised him. That same afternoon I took down a brand new notebook, cracked open its spine and under the heading 'The South', entered:

1 Scythians – Sarmatians – Alans

2 Steppe

3 Mountains

4 Cossacks

5 Old Believers

6 The Spirit-Wrestlers on the edge of the world

On the next page I wrote:

The land between the Caspian and Black Seas is Russia's
Vendée, where serfs and schismatics fled to become
Cossacks, where rebels like Stenka Razin and Pugachev
rose to march on Moscow, where the perennial urge to
conformity seems at its weakest – the place where the
sea-like flatness of the steppe breaks against the Caucasus and all its scatterings of non-Russian peoples . . .

I gathered maps and went on a round of farewell visits. I
handed back my Lenin Library card and caught a last glimpse
of Christ the Saviour (walls almost complete, towers begun),
and on a lovely sunny morning bought in advance a one-way
ticket to Rostov-on-Don.

PART I

Steppe

'I threw in everything and left for the steppes of the Bashkirs to breathe fresh air, drink koumiss and live a primitive life.'

From *A Confession* by Leo Tolstoy

The Victorious Tractor

At Moscow's Kazansky Station they were shooting a film. It was early evening and a crowd of 1930s extras was standing on the platform. A man suddenly broke out of the crowd and threw himself on the tracks. The crowd pulled back and gasped. The scene was repeated several times. It was still being repeated when the Rostov train clanked at its couplings and slid out of the station.

Moscow's half-built fringe gave way to forest. For an hour or so I watched a line of dark green trees pass before the window. Then we entered a stretch of open ground full of lakes and in the last of the light there was a monastery whose towers and cupolas rose like fireworks into the night sky.

The compartment door slid open. A policeman came in and accepted a shot of vodka from the man opposite. He sat down fatly, raised his glass and said to me: 'You know what we say about Rostov?'

'No.'

'If Odessa is the father of crime, then Rostov is the mother!' He puffed out his chest. 'But of course it is a very disciplined city. It's a Cossack city.'

I asked him to tell me about the Don Cossacks.

Smoothing down the ends of his moustache, he began to speak of the life of the Cossacks and their proud customs, about how bravely they had all fought for Russia in the old days, and how they would gather at the famous *krug* and sit around the fire telling stories of the old days and how bravely they had all fought for Russia.

'But it is not an easy life and not everyone is up to it.'

The women, he explained, used to put their babies in a snow-drift, and if the baby died then it was just as well as it proved it was too weak to live a Cossack life.

Then there was the *banya*! A true Cossack, he said, likes nothing better than a good *banya*, and before the *banya* he must run out onto the steppe and lie naked on the ant-hills. The ants crawl all over him and suck out the bad blood. 'But even the strongest of the Cossacks cannot lie on those ant-hills for more than a minute. It's those big ants, you see, like this.' He held up his thumb and index finger; there was a gap between them of more than an inch.

'And now,' the policeman stood up. 'I am required to look at your papers.'

I gave them to him.

'You have a visa for Rostov?'

'It's not necessary.'

'I will decide that!'

He flicked through the papers, paused just long enough to make his point, then slapped them back in my hand.

'So, we will drink to your journey. We will have the toast the Cossack makes before going to war, when he rides out over the hill to where his little soul is waiting for him and she lets him spend the last night with her and in the morning she sees him off again with a towel over her arm and bread and salt and a cup of vodka. And he's on his horse and he drinks to his fortunes and throws the cup to the ground. There's that toast, my friend, for a journey!'

I reached Rostov late the following day. Evening flooded the streets with its honey-coloured light. Men with sunburned faces were squatting in the dust. The Russian they spoke was slower than in Moscow and softer. Rows of poplars stretched long shadows across the tramlines, and on the corner of Budyonnov-sky Prospekt my attention was at once caught by two men – their flocculent beards, and their stomachs which swelled the tunics of their tin-soldier uniforms. This was Cossack country.

1993. Summer, late July. In the mountains of Karabakh, the Armenians had launched an offensive. All night I had watched the battle for a village near Hadrut. There was a late counter-attack by a number of Azeri tanks. It was all very noisy, very confused. But by dawn it was over; the Armenians had taken the village.

First light revealed the stumps of burning houses, the casualties, the weariness, the sudden silence. A helicopter arrived to evacuate the wounded, and from it a Cossack jumped down with a group of reinforcements. He wore cavalry top-boots, red-piped breeches and an old-fashioned white tunic. As the helicopter rose again above the trees, the Cossack's cap blew off and he chased it as it rolled across the field. He was the first Cossack I'd seen in the flesh. I asked him what he was doing there.

'I have come to protect the Motherland!'

But whose Motherland that was, I wasn't sure.

At the top of Rostov is the town's Gorky Theatre, a vast building of concrete and glass designed, in the spirit of its age, to look like a caterpillar tractor. Its tracks are walkways and lift-shafts, its engine-cover the walls of the auditorium. Until the 1930s the Armenian cathedral had stood on the site, but no one was sad when the Party blew it up as they all knew by then that cathedrals were a thing of the past, and that the future lay in caterpillar tractors, built in the glorious new Rostselmash tractor works.

In front of the Gorky Theatre the land falls away to the banks of the river Don. Beyond the river I could see yellow-brown flats and poplar groves and beyond them, the steppe. Cloud-shapes drifted over it like ships. The green of the land thinned to a straight horizon, and the impression was oceanic in its scale and symmetry.

It was the end of April. The three-day snowstorms of the winter were gone. The ground was frost-free and spongy with rain. In a week or two, the mud would dry out and the going underfoot would firm up and on the third morning or perhaps the fourth there would come on the wind the very faint sound of drumming hooves. You would watch the horizon and see nothing and tell yourself it was only the wind. Then would come the slap of a lacquered cuirass, the jangle of a crudely-forged bit and they would appear, close-packed, from the one place you hadn't looked.

For more than two thousand years the crescent of grassland that runs unbroken from the banks of the Danube to the Altai mountains was dominated by successive bands of horsemen. It was the thaw that set them moving. They never settled or sowed grain but roamed in groups of up to three thousand and attacked anything they saw. They rode short-necked ponies that could gallop for an hour without stopping, or at a moment's notice lie flat in a ditch. They rode often without stirrups and they broke the ponies to a snaffle bit. In battle the horsemen preferred mares, who could urinate at a gallop, while they themselves needed only to shift slightly in the saddle to defecate. When a horse died, they ate it.

Wave upon wave of these peoples swept west across the steppe. Conquerors became conquered. Scythians replaced Cimmerians and were themselves replaced by Sarmatians. Then came Huns and Hipchaks and Mongols, and from the thirteenth century the descendants of these invaders became generically as Tatars. In the time of the Golden Horde, the Tatars used an Arabic word, '*kazak*', or Cossack, to describe a footloose soldier, a freebooter – of which there were many. Groups of Cossacks gathered together to live on the rivers in 'stanitsas' and elect their own leader as 'ataman'. They were never an ethnic group and accepted anyone into their midst who was prepared to endure what they did.

The Cossacks lived the life of an island people. They survived by pirating, paying tribute to no one, sure in the knowledge that they knew their land better than anyone who might come to it. They could track man or beast for days, undetected, over any terrain. They could wriggle snake-like through the grass. From the flight of a bird or the cry of a crow they could tell the location of an approaching stranger, and anyone entering the region learnt quickly that the empty-looking steppe was never empty. The Cossack was inseparable from his horse, and when he became sick would leap into the saddle and gallop off in any direction until such time as his sweat ran out and became one with the sweat of his horse.

Even at the time of the Revolution, these vast southern flat-lands were still largely untamed. Cossack stanitsas were dotted along the rivers – the Don, the Kuban and the Terek. Mountain drovers colonised corners for winter grazing. Trade caravans picked their way patiently along its unmarked routes, but other-wise there was nothing but limitless tracts of silky grass swaying in the wind.

The Soviet planners saw two problems when they looked to this southern wilderness. They remembered the Civil War and General Denikin and the winter of 1918–19; they remembered the number of Whites he had mustered among the Cossacks. And they thought of food: limitless supplies of grain and meat and milk. The steppe was no more than a vast food factory just waiting for the right machinery.

The solution to each problem was the same. They built the

Gorky Theatre in its image. They built the Rostselmash works. Caterpillar tractors, marching in line across the virgin soil! Caterpillar tractors, the new warriors of the steppe!

It was the time of tulips in Rostov, waxy red tulips with flames of yellow rising from the stamen. They were brought in by village women and sold from plastic buckets in the subways. They burst out of vases on the desks of office-workers, lay like gloves on tombs, beneath icons, and had been left in great numbers before the statue of Lenin. I sat watching one being pulled to pieces, petal by petal, by a fast-talking and anxious journalist. She was telling me about a certain Cossack ataman.

'I wrote an article about him, and now he says he wants to kill me. By hanging, if I'm not mistaken.'

The journalist brushed the tulip petals from her desk and said she wasn't bothered. 'It's all bluster, just Cossack bluster. If you want to know about the Cossacks, the real Cossacks, talk to Nikolai Alekseyevich.'

I found Nikolai Alekseyevich that afternoon in a village a few miles down the Don. His dog leapt at its chain and a row of salted perch hung from his clothes line. Together we walked out of the village to visit the grave of his father.

Nikolai was a wonderfully gentle man with a long, sad face. He stood at the grave with his cap in his hands. The steppe wind tugged at his hair. For some moments we remained there in silence, facing the wafer-shaped headstone and its cameo of his half-smiling father.

'It was the camps. They took him up there with the other Cossacks. Ten years he survived. But he didn't last more than six months back here. He died the day after Stalin. I think he was just waiting.'

Recently, Nikolai had visited St Petersburg for the first time.

He had been struck in particular by the Scythian gold in the Hermitage. 'You have seen the gold?'

'Yes.'

'When I saw those gold animals, they sent vibrations through my whole body. They are *ours*, you see.'

Nikolai was in little doubt that it was the Cossacks who were the true inheritors of the Scythian legacy, and he pointed to the ground. The Cossacks of that village had chosen for their graveyard the slopes of a *kurgan*, one of the hundreds of Scythian burial mounds that break the flatness of the steppe.

'We are of the same earth.'

What little is known of Scythian lore does, at least in spirit, have something in common with the Cossacks. According to Herodotus, the Scythians were a people who lived for horses and hunting and fighting. He tells a story from the Persian wars that combines all three. Just before one of the battles, with the two armies facing each other, a hare ran between the lines. The Scythians at once broke ranks and galloped after it. So alarmed were the Persians by the Scythians' nonchalance that they promptly withdrew their forces and refused to fight.

The Scythians lived in their wagons and were constantly on the move. They knew neither hoe nor plough. Their staple was mare's milk and they believed lactation was aided by inserting a hollow bone into the vulva, and blowing. Wood being scarce, they would cook an animal over a fire of its own bones, and in battle they scalped their victims and gilded the inside of the skulls to make drinking bowls. They were great drinkers. They drank their wine unwatered, and in ancient Greece drinking to excess was to 'drink like a Scythian'. In Athens they were used as police troops. The land of the Scythians was on the northern shores of the Black Sea whose coastline, it was said, was the shape of one of their bows.

When a Scythian died, the body was drawn around on a

wagon for forty days before being taken to the place of burial. Mourners erected a tent and placed mats in it around a pit of burning coals. From time to time they threw water on the coals and the steam bathed their skin; cannabis seeds were also tossed on the coals, which made the Scythians howl with laughter. If the dead man was a king, they would cut open his stomach and fill it with flowers and then take it to a place far away. There they dug a vast and elaborate chamber into which went the strangled corpses of a concubine, a wine-bearer, a cook, a groom, a valet and a bearer of messages. Horses and cups of gold were added. Then for days the people would work to heap earth upon the grave, and sometimes the *kurgany* they built were seventy feet high. At the end of that year they would return to the site with fifty of the dead king's servants and fifty of his finest horses. They killed the men and horses and mounted the dead men on the dead horses. Then they drove wooden stakes through both and arranged them in a circle around the *kurgan*. The job complete, the Scythians leapt onto their horses and rode away across the steppe.

For a long time the Scythians controlled the territory north of the Caucasus. In the seventh century BC they rode south, single file through the mountains' only pass and, bursting out into Anatolia aroused fears that the people of Gog and Magog had arrived. For a generation they controlled the entire Near East until one night the Median king Cyaxeres floored their leaders with drink and murdered them as they slept.

To the north of the Scythians, said Herodotus, the air was full of feathers. A thousand years later it was from here that the kingdom of Rus emerged. Thwarted by the taxes and retributions of the Asiatic hordes, Russians managed in the end to break through the feathers and reach the Black Sea and the Caucasus. Only then did the Cossacks become, rather than adversaries, the protectors of all things Russian. No one now wears the reinvented emblems of Russianness more boldly than the Cossack.

When in 1918 Aleksandr Blok wrote 'Scythians', he was warning the people of Western Europe that for too long they had indulged in their soft pleasures; they had become emasculated by comfort. In the Russian Revolution though, if they looked carefully, they would detect the stirrings of an ancient zeal:

> to love as our blood loves,
> None of you has loved like that for so long!
> You have forgotten such love exists
> which burns, and destroys!

Russia has reserves of passion it can unleash at any time. Do not take us for granted, he was saying, we are the children of the hordes and we have the patience of eternity.

Historically, it's all nonsense. A thousand years separate the demise of the Scythians from the appearance of the Russians, and the Cossacks came even later. But standing on the *kurgan* with Nikolai Alekseyevich that afternoon, history seemed little more than a churlishly-added detail. Much more telling was that the Cossacks had chosen the Scythian myth at all.

'Just a little unpleasantness with some of the lads.' Ataman Vladimir flashed a smile. 'A little unpleasantness, that's all.'

Nikolai Alekseyevich had directed me on down the banks of the Don to another Cossack village. Ataman Vladimir and I were standing outside the gate of the local police station. There'd been a fight the night before and five of his 'lads' had been taken in.

'A misunderstanding with some regulars. Nothing really.' He said that sixty people had been involved.

When the gate opened, Ataman Vladimir swept through it and steered the duty officer to one side. I watched him reach into his pocket and take out some banknotes. He flashed another of his smiles and left. 'They'll be out this evening,' he told me.

Ataman Vladimir was dressed for the business of the day in a brown suit and a black shirt. He looked crisp and neat and spoke in clipped quick sentences. At his house, we sat waiting for lunch in his living room. Insignia and photographs of parades filled the shelves. There was one photograph of a man on a white horse – his great-grandfather, he said, also an ataman.

'Show him the sword, dear!' shouted his wife from the kitchen.

'The sword, yes.' Vladimir reached up for the *shashka*, a long ceremonial sword that hung on the wall against a red Caucasian carpet. He pulled it out of its scabbard and, grinning, made several quick Xs in the air. He picked up the *bulava*, the ataman's mace, his symbol of office, and a stubby little weapon of solid brass. Vladimir heaved it around: 'Uhr-uhrr!'

Also on the wall hung daggers and pistols and a knout of half-woven leather straps. This was a *nagaika*. The Scythians had used it in battle, the Kirghiz had killed leopards with it, the Cossacks took it on wolf hunts. In the pictures of the Cossack charges during the 1905 revolution it is the *nagaika* they wield. Vladimir slapped it against his leg. 'Break a man's skull with that.'

Ataman Vladimir's wife appeared with plates of food and we sat at the table. She was a plain woman who laughed easily and made very good *pelmeni* and didn't like Jews. 'I don't know why they don't all go to Israel. They just make trouble for us here.' She produced a book in which the Politburo of 1936 was listed; she had put stars against those she claimed were Jewish. 'Look – two out of three!'

'Oh my God!' Vladimir cried.

'It's the truth, my dear.'

'No.' He pulled back his sleeve. 'The medals! I have to give out the medals at two!'

It was ten past. We hurried to his car and off across the village to the school.

In the assembly hall were a dozen or so tables and sitting at them a great number of smartly-dressed veterans. An accordion player was accompanying a singer who crooned through a series of wartime songs.

Fifty years ago they'd finally defeated the fascist menace and now, all over the country, every one of those who had taken part was to be given a medal. True, there'd been many of those down here, following the purges of Kaganovich in the 1930s, who had been quite keen on the fascist menace when it arrived and did little to resist it and even joined in, but all that was forgotten now, and a pile of red medal cases lay on the table.

Ataman Vladimir stood with a colonel and dispensed the medals. The colonel made a speech and then the music started again. I went to sit at one of the tables. The men were making quick work of the brandy and the women were secreting food into their bags.

'We used to eat from American tins at the front. They were tasty, those American tins . . .'

'We fought together because we drank together . . .'

One of the women had been a telephone operator at regional headquarters. She told me how one night she had flicked a switch and a familiar voice came through the headphones. It was Stalin.

'What's your name?' he asked.

'Aleksandra – Shurochka.'

'Well, don't worry, Shurochka, victory will be ours.'

She sighed and looked around the room. 'People were better in the war. Everything else was bad, but the people were better. Now look at us. How ugly we've all become.'

*　　*　　*

Ataman Vladimir mentioned a victory parade to be held in Novocherkassk, capital of the Don Cossacks. I travelled up the day before, on an afternoon of low cloud and drizzly rain. The steppe disappeared into mist. In the Cossack museum someone told me about a so-called 'green ataman'.

I found him sitting in his kitchen with two or three others. They were discussing the dismal plight of fish in Russia. The rivers had been turned into sewers, said the ataman. The Sea of Azov was a death-trap. Russia had had the finest fish in the world, the biggest sturgeon, the most wholesome salmon, the tastiest crayfish. But the Communists had just killed them, sucked them out of the water with vacuum cleaners. The solution, he proposed, lay with the Cossacks. As in the past they had helped protect Russia's frontiers, now they could protect the environment. He saw their role as rangers of Russia's lakes and rivers – guardians of the fish. 'Always Cossacks have shown a love of Russia's wide-open spaces. Isn't it better than all this play-acting as soldiers?'

He was hoping to stand in the next parliamentary election. 'I have invented a slogan,' he said. 'It is very democratic.'

'What is the slogan?'

'"For fish! For freedom! For a better lot!"'

I wished him luck with his fish and went off to find the government hotel. During the night the rain grew heavier and in the morning it shone brightly on the cobbles in front of the cathedral. A number of Cossacks had gathered there for the parade, standing around in their mismatched and outdated uniforms. Apart from them there was no one else in the square.

Something had gone wrong. Ataman Vladimir was in anxious debate with several others. Then from somewhere far up the avenue came the sound of a marching band, and it struck the Cossacks that they'd been told to be in the wrong place.

I saw them later at the parade. They'd found a slot beside

the regulars. They were all bunched up and jostling each other. They kept breaking ranks to go for a cigarette. Behind them was the burnt-out husk of a hotel. It had been fire-bombed the previous week and its blackened timbers stuck out at strange angles above the heads of the Cossacks.

Kolkhoz Lenina

Each Sunday afternoon in Rostov-on-Don, a dozen or so elderly women tucked bundles of food under their arms, boarded trams and trolley-buses and travelled across town to congregate in front of the tractor-shaped Gorky Theatre. There in an upper room (roughly corresponding to the tractor's crank-case) they spent a few hours singing the songs and reciting the prayers which were all that remained with them from the villages.

Rain was blowing in from the steppe. One of the women was struggling with an umbrella. Another was counting heads. 'Ten, eleven, twelve – are all the girls here? Good! Then let's go in.'

The girls found the stairs something of a trial. 'Oj-oj-oj!' they sighed, and bunched up on the landings to catch their breath.

'Not far now!' said Ludmilla, who at forty or so was somewhat younger than the others.

At the top of the stairs was a room bordered by shelves of jam jars. Paintbrushes burst from them; taped to the wall were fourteen paintings of an onion. In the week a class of school-children came here to experiment with paints, and their enthusiasm had left its mark in the rainbow spatterings on the table. Ludmilla flicked open a white cloth and it settled over the table. Bags of home-produced food were placed on top of it.

The women were Doukhobors, 'spirit-wrestlers', descendants of those radical sectarians who emerged at some time in the mid-eighteenth century. They had survived Stalin's years of persecution, the treks through Russia's wide-open spaces, and now each week in Rostov they found a sanctuary of sorts in the empty recesses of this concrete tractor.

'We bother no one here,' said Ludmilla. 'And no one bothers us. Sometimes we stay until seven.'

Try and trace the Doukhobors and you soon get lost in a murk of spiritual dissent. Cousins of the flagellant Khlysty, the Skoptsy (who castrated themselves) and the Ikonobors ('icon-wrestlers'), some Doukhobors see their origins in the fiery furnace of ancient Babylon and those who stepped unscathed from within it – Shadrach, Meshach and Abednego. Others claim that the sect originated with a Romanov grand duke who renounced his position to become a peasant. It was in the 1780s though, in the region of Tambov, that the sect began to attract attention. That was the time when a man named Ilarion Pobiro-khin was wandering from village to village claiming to be the living Christ. He was sent to Siberia and never returned.

But the Doukhobors did not forget him. Ignoring what they saw as the corrupted institutions of the Church – the priesthood, the icons, the liturgy, even the scriptures – they tried to live in the way most likely to release the spark of light that lives in each individual. Like the Manichaeans before them, they used light as the central metaphor of their belief – an inner light, light equated with goodness, light trapped in the body of man. And like the dualist sects spawned by the Manichaeans – the Paulicians, the Bogomils, the Cathars – the Doukhobors were driven above all in their zeal by their contempt for priests. If the spirit was there in us all, what use were priests, who came between us and God, and charged for rites, and wore bright robes, and were hypocrites, and fought like cats behind closed doors? And what use were icons, which pinned light to a wooden board?

Such ideas bred a creed of devout simplicity. Traditionally, in the Doukhobor *sobraniye* there was no pomp, no trappings, no gildings, not even a Bible, but merely a loaf of bread, a cellar of salt and a jug of water. The Doukhobors bowed to each other on entering the *sobraniye*, and they bowed to each other when they left; they bowed when they met in the road, or in the fields; husbands bowed to wives before they went to bed, wives bowed to husbands. But above even bowing, the Doukhobors loved to sing.

Ludmilla cleared her throat. 'Now, before we start, we must congratulate Maria on her new set of teeth.'

Maria was a round-faced woman of about eighty. 'I'm shorry if I shing shtrangely, only I'm not yet ushed to them.'

A series of prayers began the *sobraniye*. A pale woman stood and recited a catechismal psalm. She swayed slightly as she delivered the phrases, each one polished smooth by generations of use. The psalm was called '*Pochemu ya dukhoborets*', 'Why I am a Doukhobor':

'Do you have a lamp?
I do.
And what is a lamp?
A lamp is the burning faith of an untainted conscience.
And do you have a temple of God?
I do.
And what is the temple of God?
Our deeds are the temple of God and our soul is the
    image of God and our prayers are the altar raised to
    God.
Why do you not believe in our images and our icons?
It is better to see clearly with one eye than to be blinded
    in both.
And what kind of a man are you?
I am a Doukhobor.

And why are you a Doukhobor?

Because having suffered, God is the spirit, God is the word and God is man.

And to what God do you pray?

He who created us and the sky and the earth, and who opened the light – to this God we pray and we bow . . .'

They then sang a lament for Mount Zion and a song called 'I Walked Out into the Field with Sorrow'.

Ludmilla sighed. 'We do sing such sad songs!'

'We sing sad songs because our lives are sad ones.'

'Let's sing "*Molodinky Kazachok*".'

'Yes! "*Molodinky Kazachok*"!'

They all agreed that '*Molodinky Kazachok*' was the one to sing. It was not a Doukhobor song but a traditional song of the steppe. It told of a roving young Cossack who spies a girl as he roves and asks her to let him in to spend the night. The girl says: no, young Cossack, I'm afraid for my reputation. And the young Cossack says: my horse won't stay here for long and nor will I – and she lets him in.

Maria said: 'Our shinging always reminds ush of the village life.'

'Our spirit was strong then and our body was strong.'

'It was a hard life but we were strong.'

'We watched the geese with our eyes, rocked the cradle with one foot, spun wool with the other . . .'

They had started to unpack their food. One or two were still humming the songs. The table was soon covered with tomatoes and spring onions and home-cooked meat cutlets. At the sight of food, their spirits lifted.

'Where are these villages?' I asked.

Ludmilla was slicing a cucumber. She gestured out of the low window with her knife. 'Out there. Out there on the Salsk steppe.'

The bus crossed the river Don and headed out into open country. Double lines of poplars bordered the road and behind them the unfenced fields stretched out towards the horizon. It was a blustery morning and the leaves of the poplars flashed in the wind.

On the bus was a Muscovite named Olga. 'Olga Petrovna,' she insisted. She talked of her flat in Moscow, a lovely flat from the Stalin period that looked out onto the statue of Mayakovsky. It was a flat awarded to her for services as a journalist. 'But they stole my flat, those philistines who run our country.' She was staying now with her sister in Salsk, just for the time being. She didn't like Salsk; she wanted to be back in Moscow.

'You have read, I suppose, some of our Russian writers?' she asked.

'A few.'

'Which?'

'Pushkin, Tolstoy –'

'Tolstoy,' she scoffed. 'What he does to our language! Writing like a German with those great long sentences. But of course, Pushkin, he is the great one. Which others?'

'Turgenev.'

'He is good.'

'Zamyatin.'

'Excellent.'

'And Dostoevsky.'

'No. Dostoevsky had good ideas, but he couldn't get them down properly. A clumsy writer.'

'Pasternak?'

'Pasternak wrote some good poetry – but *Zhivago* is a metro romance.'

'Mandelstam –'

'Wrote a poor Russian. Always aware of what effect he was having.'

'Tsvetaeva –'

'Yes. Though a woman.'

'Akhmatova –'

'A woman! You have read Bunin?'

'No.'

'He was a great one. Babel?'

'Yes.'

'He had great spirit.'

'And you,' I asked her. 'Who do you rate most highly?'

She looked up, placing one hand against her throat. 'For me there is one above all, and that is Mayakovsky. He was such a big man, a great tall man! When you read the poems of Mayakovsky it's as if the words are falling from him like rain. To him, everything was possible.'

And from her bag she pulled a photograph, a creased black-and-white photograph of the statue of Mayakovsky which had appeared against the distant rooftops of her Moscow skyline. He stands like the literary warrior he was, the 'cloud in trousers', larger than life, ready to do battle with the old guard and fulfil all the brilliant hopes of the Revolution.

Vladimir Mayakovsky shot himself in 1930.

Salsk was dust and dirt and the hutch-like shapes of Soviet provincial architecture. I watched Olga Petrovna as she crossed to the market stalls. She was bending to pick some peonies from a bucket when a dog appeared suddenly at her feet. The dog barked. Olga stepped backwards in shock. She flustered about for some moments. The last I saw of her she was hurrying away down a side-street, the peonies cradled to her chest.

In the mid-afternoon, another bus bounced out of Salsk along a half-metalled road. On the dashboard was a sleeping cat. An old man was singing behind me. After an hour or so the driver called over his shoulder: 'Kolkhoz Lenina!'

I slammed the door and the bus pulled away. I watched it shrink into the distance. Silence. A wind came out of the fields and brought with it the smell of wormwood and new growth. The ground was soft but the edges of the ruts were already crusted and pale. I struck out along the road for the first village.

The Doukhobor villages – Brigades 1 to 5 of the Kolkhoz Lenina – were strung like beads along a straight and narrow road, each one a few kilometres from the last. There had been a time in the late 1920s when straight lines were seen as the answer to everything, when the kolkhoz planners dreamed dreams of three harvests a year and mechanical devices that would do it all for them. Within a season or two the peasants would be leaving the land for the towns to assist in the great flowering of Soviet industry. In Marx's view, the peasantry were as redundant a class as capitalists.

In Brigade 2, the Polyarkovs were preparing for a party. Their daughter, Natalya, was sixteen that day and her father was killing a pig. He raised one bloodied hand and ushered me in. The party went on long into the night. We ate at a long table in the yard and danced by the pig-pen. Morning hoisted a hazy sun above the fields and brought Natalya's friends spilling out of the hay-lofts, in pairs out of the byre, shaking the straw from their hair.

'I can't think what they've all been doing,' said her grandmother.

I asked her what she remembered of the thirties and she laughed. 'It's no good asking me, I can't remember anything any more.' She flicked her stick up the road. 'Go and see Fyodor Mikhailovich. Third Brigade.'

I set off down the road in good spirits. Brigade 2 was audible a long time after I'd left it – its barking dogs, its lowing beasts, the endless debates of its crowing cocks. But after a while there was just the wind around my ears. On either side of the road were fields of rye and great double stands of elm which had been planted in the 1930s and now criss-crossed the steppe like outsize hedges. From the air, I thought, it must look like some giant check tablecloth.

In Brigade 3 I waited in the prayer house for Fyodor Mikhailovich. Cherry trees and apple trees stood outside in the orchard. Inside the door was the list of Doukhobors who'd disappeared in Stalin's purges, and in the corner usually reserved in Russian houses for the icon was a bust of Tolstoy.

Tolstoy and the Doukhobors were natural allies. To him, these stubborn peasants were the embodiment of his idea of 'Christian anarchy'. He saw in them a group who lived not by the rules of state or Church, who worshipped not according to some tired or coercive tradition, but in response to the spirit or light within them. In 1895, they won him over completely by their dogged resistance to conscription and the savage persecutions they endured. Tolstoy himself was already under close scrutiny by the authorities. His only recourse was to report the persecutions abroad, by means of an anonymous article in the London *Times*.

It is hard to know exactly how much the Doukhobors affected the restless thinking of Tolstoy. But on the day he wrote the article, his diary reveals their ideas creeping into his language: 'Everyone sins in proportion to the light in him.'

Later, Tolstoy heard a rumour that he was in the running for the first-ever Nobel Prize. He wrote at once to the Swedish press, proposing that the award should be given not to him but to the Doukhobors. In the end neither got it, but Tolstoy did give them the proceeds from his story *Resurrection*, which helped many of them to reach Canada, where they became well known for marching naked in support of their beliefs.

'There you are!'

I turned round from Tolstoy. Fyodor Mikhailovich was standing in the doorway of the prayer house. He bowed deeply to me. 'My wife, she also wants to say hello.' He added another deep bow. 'That one's from her!'

I warmed at once to Fyodor Mikhailovich. He had a thick moustache with curly ends, and a tall hat that made him look like an early pioneer of the American West. I sat with him all morning in the prayer house, and when the women of Brigade 3 came to sing some psalms, and Fyodor Mikhailovich sat listening to them with his hands resting on the polished top of his cane, his face remained full of laughter. On occasions he would raise his head and squint as if trying to make out some distant object. But it was his eyes, he said, they'd been burnt by the Siberian sun.

Fyodor Mikhailovich had clear ideas about what it meant to be a Doukhobor and dotted his conversation with the simple axioms by which he had always tried to live.

'If we don't love each other, we kill God ... What we sow we shall reap ... Christ was a *muzhik* ...'

He'd also thought a good deal about his origins, and concluded that in the beginning the world was stone, then the sun warmed it up and out crawled 'a whole lot of them wormy things'. He was no Creationist and believed that after that, progress towards man with 'his consciousness and thoughts' was pretty much inevitable.

'Man's soul, it's like a nut, you see. The shell might disappear but what's inside goes on for ever. Goes to make new trees and new nuts.'

Fyodor Mikhailovich had been ten when his group of Doukhobors crossed the Caucasus from Georgia. It was the time after the Civil War and there was famine. He remembered the people coming up to the wagons to beg for food and sometimes their bodies lying beside the road. In Maikop, the Doukhobor elders obtained permission from Lenin to settle land in the Salsk steppe.

'There was grass up to here then,' Fyodor raised the point of his cane. 'You could ride a horse through it without being seen. Lovely land it was, but full of little beasts, buzzing and creeping and mice everywhere. You'd wake up and wipe the little devils out of your hair. Those first winters we nearly died with the cold. And in the summer, the heat was like an oven. But the worst of it was that filth –' He stopped abruptly.

'What filth?'

'That filth that bites. What's it called?'

'Mosquitoes?'

'Yes . . . no! Big teeth, like dogs . . .'

'Wolves?'

'Wolves, that's the one. Wolves at night howling like the devil.'

All through the 1920s the Doukhobors struggled with the land. Each winter took its toll – the old and the sick and the very young. By the spring they'd have only seed grain left or cattle-feed to eat, and the herds starved. They had few contacts with the outside world. Yet within ten years, after a couple of good harvests, they had built up a surplus. They managed to construct barns and buy new stock, and with elaborately-carved bargeboards they decorated the prayer house.

Then, on a day of bright sunshine, the activists came in from Salsk.

Fyodor remembered their arrival. They came on bicycles. They wore dark shirts buttoned up to the neck.

'Where are your poor people?' they demanded.

'Poor people? We don't have no poor people,' said the Dou-khobors. 'We're a community.'

'You must have poor people. Everyone has poor people.'

The activists looked around the houses and they found one old man without shoes and they said to him: 'When we're rid of these kulaks, you'll have all the shoes you need.'

The activists came again a year or so later. They called a meeting. They explained that villages like this one were part of a great big idea that was sweeping the world. It involved pooling their labour and pooling their livestock. The Doukhobors were not too sure about that. Things worked well enough as they were, and anyway they had their own idea and one day everyone was going to live as *they* did. Didn't Lenin himself say that 'Doukhoborism is spiritual communism'?

That's as may be, said the cadres, who had their quotas to think about. They pointed out into the steppe and said: 'When you join the collective farm we will build tramways between your villages. Collective farms are the path to prosperity – trac-tors will conquer the steppe.'

The meeting took place in the assembly hall. When the speeches ended, someone started playing the accordion. The people were required to walk up to the front and say: 'I am so-and-so and I declare myself a member of the Kolkhoz Lenina.'

When it came to Fyodor's turn he walked up and said: 'Look, my brothers are working in the fields and I do not have the right to talk for them . . .'

'Get on with it!'

'Well, to tell you the truth,' said young Fyodor, 'I don't know about this kolkhoz. The way I see it is we work well enough now and we look after our beasts. I don't see why we must –'

'Get him out!'

Outside he was arrested at once. After interrogation they

sentenced him to five years under Article 58 of the Soviet constitution.

Fyodor looked down at the ground and leaned on his stick.
'We went into Rostov and in the prison it was full up but I
found some other Doukhobors there. We sang some psalms
and felt better. I even made up my own poem there.'

I asked him if he remembered the poem. He cleared his
throat and fixed me with his benevolent stare:

'We were born across the Caucasus,
And we grew up on the Salsk steppe.
We were brought up in the communal life,
And we bore many trials.
We didn't learn to steal,
Or rob other people or betray them.
But evil people came and wrote clauses,
And the evil people clouded everything with their clauses,
And with that they took us away,
And put us in this stinking cellar.
Here we sit in our prison and peer through the bars,
And we do not see our loved ones,
And our hearts have grown sick,
And our faces are streaming with bitter tears,
And we know no one except the guard.'

Fyodor Mikhailovich chewed for a moment on his
moustache.

'What happened then, Fyodor?'

'Took us north. To the furthest place they knew about.
There's another poem I wrote about that. Will you hear it?'

'Please.'

'Put us in trucks and we didn't know where they took us.
We only knew when we arrived at Kotlas.

And at Kotlas they called us out,
And they announced our sentences.
Some people eight years, some people ten.
So they announced our sentences,
And put us in the hold of a boat,
And the ruffians tormented us and beat us,
And they took away even the last piece of our belongings,
And they gave us no rest.
To work we walked weak and blind.
And we didn't even earn bread.
And we lay down hungry and slept.'

Fyodor looked around the room. The midday sun was slant-ing through the window. 'I ate up all my teeth in the north. Turnips we were given hard as rock. In the summer the sun made us blind, but I had all our Doukhobor prayers and psalms and they kept me alive.'

On a March morning several years later Fyodor arrived back in Brigade 3. The steppe was unchanged, and Fyodor said he felt 'the joy of love' to be back in the village after so long. But the land was now collectivised and there was no place for him. 'They said I was an enemy of the people.'

He found others in the same position and they asked each other: 'What can we do?' They debated the matter and agreed that if nothing was done they would soon starve. They sent a petition to the Regional Committee, saying: 'The spring has begun and we must sow in order that we can feed ourselves. Please, we need land!'

The Regional Committee replied: 'The land has been granted to the people for the everlasting use of the kolkhoz. *You* are not even allowed to walk on it.'

So they gathered together again and said: 'If we don't do something we won't even see the winter.'

There was silence. Then Fyodor said: 'Wait. Isn't it right that the earth belongs to the people?'

'It's what they say.'

'Well, aren't we the people just like everyone else?'

They all agreed he was right, so they sent another petition. Again they were turned down. They met to discuss it and said there was only one thing they could do. Two of them volunteered to go and see Kalinin in Moscow. They would tell him what was happening. He would help, once he knew what was happening in their village!

Fyodor could still remember the wording of the petition.

'We're a group of peasants,' it read. 'We need to live on something. Lenin gave us this land and now it's been taken away. What can we do, Comrade Kalinin? It seems that some bad people have come to our region and are stopping us from being on the land.'

They went into Salsk and saw the two men off on the train. They waited two weeks, a month. After six months, they wrote a letter to Moscow to see what had happened. They waited for the reply but after two weeks there was none, nor after a month. They never received a reply, and no one ever heard of those poor petitioners again.

'They just showed them in one door, and showed them out of another.'

Later Fyodor invited me to have lunch in his home. The village was just one muddy road and a row of clapboard cabins built end-on down each side. We walked slowly and Fyodor looked at all of the budding trees and sometimes he prodded the ground in a proprietorial way. Each person we passed greeted him. 'Good day, Fyodor Mikhailovich!' He bowed in response.

Fyodor sat at the head of the table in silence while we ate, and after we'd eaten I pulled out a map and asked him to show me where he was born. We found the lake where he'd swum as a boy in the Wet Mountains of Georgia, and we found the village of Goryelovka.

I told him it was there that I was headed.

'That was where they burnt the guns,' he said.

The burning of the guns, in June 1895, was the defining act of the Doukhobors. Rather than answer the Tsar's call to serve in the army, they had gathered all their guns together and burnt them. It was for this act that Tolstoy had fought their cause.

Fyodor's eyes wandered over the map but it wasn't at all an easy thing to read. He knew the Salsk steppe and he knew the Wet Mountains and the camps in the far north. But that was about it.

'Anywhere else, Fyodor? Have you ever been anywhere else?'

He shook his head. 'Except Volgograd once. I was in Volgograd.' Fyodor put aside the map and, smiling, dovetailed his hands in front of his stomach.

It was 1963 and the trade union had arranged an excursion for the workers of Kolkhoz Lenina. Fyodor was now in the kolkhoz and they'd exceeded their quotas. On a beautiful sunny morning, the Doukhobors all gathered in the Palace of Culture in Brigade 2. There they had a little drink before they left. Then they climbed onto the bus. The singing started on the way to the station. On the platform they were singing and the people of Tselina came out onto the street and said: Please don't stop! We like your singing!

Then the train took them off and they were singing on the train. They stayed in Volgograd for three days and saw the statue of Mother Russia – fifty metres high! Eight thousand tonnes! Her sword twenty metres long! And for the three days they were in Volgograd they were singing all the time. On the train home they were singing. They sang in the afternoon and they were singing in the evening and at last the concierge came and said: Look, you must stop your singing. The people here must have a little rest.

So the Doukhobors lay down and were quiet for a while and slept. And when they woke up again it was light and they saw the beginnings of the Salsk steppe. They were almost home, so they started singing again and when they got back home, they went from house to house singing.

'And do you know,' Fyodor chuckled, 'that in all that group not one of us had a hoarse voice.'

The next morning was bright and warm. I left Fyodor Mikhailovich sitting on a bench outside his gate. He was waiting for something to happen so that he could watch it. Nothing had happened yet and it probably wouldn't that day. He stood and bowed as I passed and said: 'Good wishes!'

I set off towards the last brigade of the line. The Doukhobors had called it Tambovka, a name which they had kept like a family photograph throughout their two-hundred-year odyssey, propping it up wherever they came to rest. There was Tambovka in the Transcaucasus and Tambovka here – and it was in the Tambov region that Ilarion Pobirokhin had first brought the Doukhobors to public notice. Tambov was famously fertile ground for prophets, chiliasts and latter-day Christs and had thus earned itself the nickname *Tambog* ('there is God').

This village of Tambovka was now practically deserted. Only every third house was standing. The rest were leafy tangles of honeysuckle and lilac. The street had about it the look of a sparsely-toothed grin. Into the abandoned houses had moved Armenians fleeing wars and earthquakes, and a man from Gyumri showed me his new potato patch and the chervil rings his wife had made. He had bought the house from a Doukhobor whose sister had died. Pointing up the street, he said: 'There is still a Doukhoborka. Her name is Maria Mikhailovna. She is the last one.'

Maria Mikhailovna was kneeling among a group of peonies. She stood slowly when she saw me and wiped her hands on her apron. When she spoke it was with the soft detachment of one used to living a long way from speech.

'Perhaps you have heard, they are saying that Stalin did certain things at that time. They say that he took people away.'

'You too?'

She looked down. 'They were arresting everyone then. Women were crying in the street.'

'And you?'

'The kolkhoz. They took my uncle. He had small children. My aunt and my mother said you mustn't take him, but they took him.'

She crossed the yard and returned with a bowl of apples. I took one and she looked at me for the first time. Her eyes were the deepest blue. 'They took me with my mother and my sister. They used to arrest people for nothing. There were twenty-seven women from this village. I worked in the camps for seven years. Did you know they had labour camps in those days?'

'I've heard.'

Maria Mikhailovna gazed out across the plain; the low sun was bright on her face. Slowly the details of her life came drifting out: of how she was born in Tambovka in Georgia, among 'those wild people' – Georgians and Armenians and Turks; and how she'd moved away from them to this new Tambovka as a girl; and how her father died young and left her with her uncle; and at seventeen she'd gone to the camps and for seven years knew nothing of the world until one day a Red Cross tin arrived and inside it was the first meat she'd eaten since her arrest. She was told the Americans were helping in the war and that soon it would be over. Then somehow when she'd returned to the village, with nothing, she'd lived alone while one by one every-one married and moved away and she'd never got around to doing either. Now the old ones had died off and she was the last one and recently, in the last years, 'those wild people' from the south had started to move in.

She stood at the fence to see me off. She looked up the road to where the Armenians were shovelling gravel from a cart. 'This village used to be so pretty, the pride of the line.'

Out on the steppe again, it was evening. I followed a grass-centred track back towards the main road. When the sun dropped through the bottom of the clouds, its brilliance came so abruptly that I stopped for a moment and squinted towards it. In the distance, shadowed by the trees, I made out a man cantering away from me on a black horse. He was standing in the saddle. His arms were working backwards and forwards along the horse's neck. He rode clear of the trees and was briefly illuminated before the horse's legs disappeared and he was taken away, dropping down beneath the horizon.

How to Build a Church in
One Night

The Doukhobors knew an Old Believer named Victor Stepanovich who lived in the local town of Tselina, on the fifth floor of a run-down apartment block. He spoke in a thick and modulated voice which would, on occasions, suddenly break out into song. His sitting-room was a thieves' den of icons and antiquities and while I waited there, a muttering and singing drifted out of the kitchen along with the rattle of cups and plates.

Victor Stepanovich was a collector. All his life he had collected. He had collected china and icons and books, pre-Revolutionary candlesticks and clocks from the West, little enamel pill-boxes and threadbare Caucasian rugs. He had collected anything he could find that was old. Collecting had been his hedge against a world that seemed intent on destroying its past. Once in the 1930s, during 'the war against the churches', he had gone to the river Don and parted the reeds to see the Vladimir Virgin staring up at him from the water.

'That year the river was full of icons. They took them from the churches and threw them in and I went down to watch them floating to the sea. So sad. I blessed each one as it passed. Farewell, brother! [singing] *Farewell brother, fare-are-are-well!*'

Collecting had also been Victor Stepanovich's downfall. His neighbour knew he was an Old Believer and tipped off the authorities. One night Victor had opened his door to the NKVD. They found his flat full of icons and silver, and he'd spent five years bending his back in a Siberian bauxite mine.

Victor Stepanovich's flat was again full of icons and silver. He sat in a cane chair, happily scooping tinned salmon into the bit of beard that was his mouth. When he smiled, the gold of his teeth showed through the beard and matched the gilding of the icons behind him. He sang too, between salmon bites. And between the salmon bites and the singing, he talked about the *kriuvka* system of musical notation, about the eight-voiced chanting retained by the Old Believers, while at the same time showing how each syllable could ride a sea of syncopations and stresses, canticle swells and pitch changes – now soft, now loud, now plaintive, now assertive. ' ... *go-o-os-po-o-o-odi-i-i-i* ... *po-o-o-omi-lu-u-ui-i-i-i* ... '

When he'd finished I asked him about the schism. But what appeared to be the end of the chant was in fact only a quiet passage: he raised the two middle fingers of his right hand.

The fingers, of course. It all came down to the fingers. When in 1653 Patriarch Nikon had tried to reform the Church he decreed that using three fingers rather than two was the ancient and proper way for supplicants to bless and cross themselves. In fact, three fingers were no more 'authentic' than two, but that didn't bother the crusading Nikon, and thereafter fingers became the emblem of the schism.

In the persecutions that followed, Old Believers had their right arm severed for maintaining the old form. Many asked to take the limb away, and noted with some satisfaction that even when lifeless the fingers held the blessing for three days. Others chose to slice off their own index finger. Surikov's celebrated picture of the Old Believer Boyarina Morozova centres on her fingers, raised in the old way, as she is dragged through the snow to her death.

Whenever the schism came up, it was always the fingers. Fingers were the schism's shibboleth. But to me it didn't quite ring true. The Doukhobors liked to say that crossing yourself is just 'brushing away the flies', and as an explanation for the round of martyrdom that followed the reforms, the tens of thousands who withdrew into the Siberian wastes, the congregations who burned themselves to death in their own churches, the two-finger/three-finger debate seems a little thin.

When Victor Stepanovich finished his singing, I said: 'But the fingers – isn't this all on the surface?'

A smile showed through the portcullis of his beard. 'No. The ritual is everything to us. The two fingers raised – like this – they are God as Father and God as Son. And here, we bend slightly the second one to show it was the Son that died on the Cross. The other three fingers, down, are the Trinity. So, you see, in one hand is the whole of our belief. The ritual is everything . . .'

It was ritual, not dogma, he explained, that had made the schism. They called themselves not '*Starovertsi*' – Old Believers, but '*Staroobryadtsi*' – Old Ritualists. Lose the ritual and everything else would follow. Ritual was the repetitive chant of their everyday actions. It added meaning and rhythm to their lives, gave contours to the flat days, erected borders to defend them from the eternal expanse all around them. Break the ritual, and the demons could come galloping in from the steppe; change the words, and the formula was gone. With Nikon's reforms, worldliness and foreign wizardry had barged into the sanctum, and the Old Believers would have nothing to do with it.

Victor Stepanovich stood. For a moment he was lost in the darkness at the back of the room. He returned with a large psalter and rested it in his lap. He wiped the dust from its worm-gnawed covers. It dated from 1645, just a few years before the schism.

'It may not seem much to you, but the words, they are like a path to us. If you change the words we lose our way.'

In the dusty villages of old Russia, notions of Church and state never really meant as much as the direct allegiance to God. Dissent broke out at the merest hint of change, and faith was clutched as a firebrand against it. When it comes to displays of religious zeal, few places come close to provincial Russia in the sixteenth and seventeenth centuries.

At the centre of it all was fasting, the rigid calendar of abstinence. During the year's four great fasts many peasants managed to starve themselves to death. When the Church authorities urged restraint, the people only accused them of heresy and fasted all the more. It was not unknown for entire villages to set off into the forest at night with axes and candles and to build a church in order to celebrate a mass by dawn. Much admired was the practice of '*stolpnichestvo*' – the ability to stay stock-still for days on end; Ilya of Murom didn't budge for thirty years. Gatherings of any kind were accompanied by readings from the sacred compendium *Cheti Mnei*, twenty-seven thousand pages long.

Most could not read the various texts that were circulating at the time, but they could listen. And by converting each letter into a numerical value, prayers became formulae. An obsession with numbers pervaded everything from the interpretation of news to the keeping of pigs.

During the fifteenth century it became increasingly clear to many Russians that the world was about to end. According to the teaching of St Cyril, the chapter of earthly existence began with Adam in 5508 BC and was due to continue for seven thousand years – the time needed for a hundred truly good souls to live and replace the hundred fallen angels. Literalists eagerly awaited the year 1492. That it passed without incident did nothing to dampen the millenarian fervour. (Had they known then the significance of Columbus's discovery of America, or the repercussions of the Spanish driving out the Moors, perhaps the Parousia would have been declared at once.) Instead a new temporal horizon was found: the Christian millennium plus the number of the Beast, the year 1666.

For four centuries devotional texts like *The Golden Chain*, *The Golden Stream* and *Pearl* had been using the apocalyptic tones of St John the Divine to remind Russians that time was finite, that all worldly sufferings and worldly joys would one day come to an end. In *Emerald* II, Chapter 162, can be found this warning:

> And then there will be no more laughter nor tale-telling
> among you nor any devilish amusements, there will be
> no swift steeds nor fine garments and you will fall down
> in death-throes ... Earth will cry as a beautiful maid
> ... and then the Antichrist will come ...

Such sentiments had begun to take root with the Mongol invasions of the thirteenth century. The forces of Gog and Magog were at large on the southern steppe, and doom-shadowed Russians learnt to find solace in the darker passages of biblical prophecy. The Book of Daniel and Revelations were particularly comforting, assuring all those who had faith that defeat of the heathen hordes would usher in the final judgement, a new heaven and a new earth, and a new Jerusalem.

It was Ivan Grozny ('the Terrible') who at Kazan achieved the decisive victory over the Mongol dynasty, the Tatar Khans. To commemorate it he built that most bizarrely Russian of all buildings, St Basil's cathedral in Red Square, which Napoleon referred to as 'that mosque'. It was dedicated to Basil the Blessed, one of the great holy fools of medieval Russia. 'Idiotic for Christ's sake', Basil was well known for wandering naked around

Moscow and throwing stones at the houses of the good while kissing the walls of sinners. He was openly critical of the tsar and prophesied, correctly, that Ivan would murder his own son. It was to Basil that Ivan attributed his victory at Kazan.

Ivan is seen as the father of the savagery with which the Russian state has always treated its people. Yet he himself claimed to be no more than a humble monk, who surrounded himself with a coterie of devout churchmen, took frequent barefoot pilgrimages and with his *Domostroy* ('Domestic Book') created a code of Leviticus-type laws that dictated the Godly way Russians must lead their lives.

And throughout these vivid, smouldering centuries the conviction grew that the Russians were the people chosen by God; that as the Third Rome, Moscow would one day come to rule all the nations of the earth; that with the fall of Byzantium to the Turks the mantle of Orthodoxy had passed to the Slavs, bringing to them the destiny not only of Constantine's capital, and of Rome, but since the Arab invasion of AD 638, that of Jerusalem too.

The Byzantine double-headed eagle had already been adopted by Muscovy as the imperial seal. And in 1472, shortly after the fall of Constantinople, the bloodline too had passed to Russia when Ivan III married the Byzantine emperor's twenty-five-stone niece. Zoe-Sophia Paleologus brought to this small princedom of the north the weight of a thousand years of theocratic tradition, and on her first night in the Kremlin the traditional bed of the grand duchesses collapsed beneath her.

Now, just outside the Kremlin walls, across Red Square from the jester's-hat cupolas of St Basil's cathedral, stands the tomb of the last pretender to Russia's Messianic throne. Lenin also promised a new Jerusalem, a new heaven on earth, salvation for the dispossessed, damnation for the tyrants. His creed would overturn the falsehood of centuries, and from Russia the forces of good would radiate around the globe and usher in the thousand-year reign of the righteous.

Victor Stepanovich said there was someone I ought to meet, a fellow Old Believer who lived in a small cabin on the edge of town.

The evening was humid; the leaves hung limp and heavy on the poplars. Pyotr Maksimovich was in his garden working at a patch of potatoes. His long hair was gathered in a cap of plastic netting. He wore no shirt and had a thin, ascetic torso. When we talked, he sat somehow twisted on a stool and stared at me from a face of vivid contrasts – the white of his skin, the black of his beard, the milky blue of his deep-set eyes.

Pyotr had been brought up in Siberia. For the first ten years of his life he knew nothing beyond three Old Believer houses built deep in the taiga. His parents had fled there in 1929 to 'save their souls and escape the Godless kolkhoz'. They took with them only a trunk of pre-*raskol* texts, and ate what they grew. When Pyotr first went downriver to the town he tried to follow the faces in the market and remembered being overcome with dizziness. He arrived on the Salsk steppe 'by certain routes' and was now concerned above all with the prophecies in a book called *Russia Before the Second Coming of Christ.*

'In the world now, everything depends on Russia.' He spoke quietly and without movement. 'This whole century, no other country on the earth has had such a role as Russia. If Russia does not repent now for the sins of the Revolution, for killing the tsar, for all this Godless destruction, the apocalypse is not far away. Russia will flourish for fifteen years, the Churches will unite. Then will be the time of the Antichrist.'

I threw in a lame comment about unfulfilled prophecies, and he calmly quoted the case of Serafim Zarovsky, who had seen the Virgin twelve times, could walk across rivers, and before his death in 1833 had prophesied not only the 1917 Revolution, but that of 1905 too. It was said that Nicholas II read the prophecy after his coronation and remained haunted by it.

Pyotr Maksimovich had studied Hebrew and Greek in order better to understand the event which had cast the Old Believers into the wilderness. He saw the schism as the single most important event in Russian history, and I saw no reason to disagree. If nothing else, it reveals most starkly those perennial Russian dilemmas: strength from beyond the frontiers versus strength from within; Westernisers versus Slavophiles; Russia as the sister of nations versus her God-given destiny.

In the years leading up to 1666 there was plenty to suggest that some revelation was at hand. Wild-eyed anchorites were stepping out of the forest to tell of their visions: '. . . the condemned will be devoured in the churches . . . the tsar is a horn of the Antichrist . . .' The Time of Troubles had left the land ravaged by Poles and Lithuanians and Swedes. Plague and revolt had swept in after them. In large areas there were ten women to every man. Bands of scavenging peasants roamed through the snow, eating each other when they could find nothing else. On one night in the winter of 1660, four thousand wolves burst into the town of Smolensk and feasted on its inhabitants.

Just as voracious were the popish foreigners who swarmed in to take advantage of the ailing Motherland. Icons began to be painted with the well-fed faces of Western portraiture. From time to time, mobs would sack the foreign district of Moscow and lynch the residents. To re-establish authority, the young Tsar Aleksei came to depend on Nikon, a fiercely devout monk who at six foot six stalks the period like an Old Testament prophet. In 1652 Nikon became patriarch, and began to receive letters from the Kremlin addressed to 'the great sun', and signed 'your earthly tsar'. On Palm Sunday, Tsar Aleksei led Nikon into Red Square on a donkey.

Nikon responded in kind. He was already endowed with the dangerous convictions of a zealot. When all three of his children died young, he had told his wife she must enter a convent. He himself walked north to become a hermit on the White Sea. Once appointed patriarch, he embarked on a rigorous campaign to purge the Church of its corruptions. He displayed in public, like criminals, the 'Frankish' icons. With his own hands he scraped away their eyes. He was deeply impressed by the writings of Arseny Sukhanov, who had recently returned from the Holy Land and Jerusalem with tales of its heretical fawning to the Turks. And it became clear to Nikon that Moscow really was the only city worthy of God's name, the true heir of Orthodoxy.

'Though I am Russian,' he announced, 'I am in faith and convictions a Greek.' He began to convert his own fundamentalism into policy. Cowls, ambos, hymns and rites arrived in Moscow from the old Orthodox world; the traditional two fingers of the blessing were replaced by three; the three 'Allelujahs' were replaced by two; the spelling of Jesus was changed (and as for many this was the only word they could read, it confirmed Nikon's campaign as a Satanic conspiracy).

A vicious epidemic of bubonic plague followed the reforms. It was found that if the numerical value of the letters of Nikon, Aleksei and Arseny were added together they came to 666; likewise the tsar's new title of Imperator. Various new texts were found to have exactly 666 pages. 'Russia' written backwards was Assur, condemned by the prophets, and those who became known as the Old Believers grew to realise what was happening, that the time was upon them, that the worldly state had ravaged their Church and that they must wait in quiet obeisance until the Second Coming.

Though his reforms stuck, Nikon himself was soon rejected. Finally snubbed by the tsar, he slipped into the vestry during a service, discarded his patriarchal alb, and left through a side door in the garb of a common mendicant. His last retreat was an island he built himself by massing vast stones in a lake.

No one knows how many dissenters Nikon created, nor how they spread over the coming years, but during the nineteenth century it was said that two out of every three merchants in Russia were Old Believers. One estimate puts the pre-Revolutionary numbers at more than ten million.

When I first asked about them in Moscow, I was told that the Old Believers were all dead. Then I met Sergei in the Lenin Library and he said no, there are many of us left but none in the south. Yet Sergei put me on to someone who knew an Old Believer priest in Rostov. When I was in Rostov I went to see him, but he had died four years earlier.

Now I asked Pyotr Maksimovich if he knew of any communities in the south that had survived. He smiled: 'What do you expect, that we are a whole nation?'

But he had heard tell of a group nearby, a literate community and a devout one.

'Where?' I asked him.

'Primorsko-Akhtarsk.'

But where that was, he had no idea.

I went to the bus station in the morning and they didn't know either. It was early and the ticket office was closed. I sat down outside to wait. In front of me was a stall selling fruit, and the stall-holder was talking to two women on a bench. All three were elderly.

> *Man:* You know, it's interesting.
> *Woman 1:* What is?
> *Man:* In the Bible –
> *Woman 1:* Pfah!
> *Man:* No, listen. I was reading it and it said in
> there that Christ was God.

Woman 1: Of course he was God.

Man: But if he was the son of Mary, how can he be God too?

Woman 1: Mary was a god.

Man: She was never a god.

Woman 1: Of course she was a god.

Man: How can Christ be a man if he was a god?

Woman 1: Who says he was a man?

Man: In the Bible –

Woman 1 (angry): How do they know? They're just lying!

Woman 2 (with a sigh): That's right. Always trying to muddle your head up with new ideas.

There was silence for a moment between the three of them. A wind came out of the steppe and sent the stall's cloth billowing over the counter. The man weighed it down with stones.

Man: It's like those men on the moon –

Woman 1 (scoffing): The moon!

Woman 2: It wasn't the moon at all. They just sent them somewhere and said it was the moon.

Man: Kazakhstan it was –

Woman 1: What nonsense . . .

Silence again.

Woman 1: It's all his fault.

Man: Who?

Woman 1: Gorbachev.

Man: I've heard people say that Gorbachev was a good man.

Woman 2: He was worse than Stalin.

Woman 1: So Stalin was pleasant now, was he?

Woman 2: He was strong. Not like these jokers
    nowadays.

Man (chuckling): In the Bible there's a story
    about –

Woman 1: A pleasant old man, eh? Killing
    people, starving them to death?

Woman 2: They're starving again now. They say
    there's famine in the Alexandrovsk region.

Man: In the Bible –

Woman 1: So it's worse than Stalin's time now?

Woman 2: That was sabotage.

Man: In the Bible, they say you can even jump
    from a high tower and live if you believe. All
    you need to do is believe.

Woman 1: Well, they're lying!

Woman 2: Just trying to muddle up your head.

When I asked them if they knew about Primorsko-Akhtarsk,
the first woman said there was no such place. The second
woman said she'd heard of it and perhaps it was in the Stavropol
region, or possibly Siberia. The man said it was full of criminals,
though he didn't know where it was either.

When the ticket office opened, a woman gestured to a sorry-
looking vehicle and said that it was due to leave in exactly five
minutes.

A Little Miracle

Primorsko-Akhtarsk turned out to be a town of some thirty thousand people, not in Siberia nor in the Stavropol region but spread along the shores of the Sea of Azov. In the early evening, grey-brown cloud hung over the coast like a fog. A cream-painted building stood near the beach, the town's only hotel. In the rooms, flies revolved in the thundery air. The bar was hot and empty. I sat in the corner with a bottle of beer and a copy of Leskov's *The Enchanted Wanderer*.

Although many of Leskov's stories concern Old Believers, *The Enchanted Wanderer* is simply a meandering picaresque tale. Only towards the end does it emerge as a rather loose allegory of Russian history. The wanderer begins the story with nothing but a mystical gift for training horses. By accident he kills a monk and as penance is forced to wander, searching everywhere for the solace of his own death. Down near the Caspian, he is captured by Tatars who cut open the soles of his feet and insert horsehair to prevent him from escaping. When, years later, he does manage to get away he becomes a drinker, is cured by a degenerate prince, falls for a gypsy girl, kills her, spends fifteen years as a soldier in the Caucasus, becomes a monk, and is in the end given the gift of prophecy by the saints Zosima and Savaty. In his vision he sees a war in which he will at last manage to die, fighting for the Russian people.

I put the book to one side and fetched another drink. A group of men swaggered into the bar – small-time hoods on a spree. They wore sleeveless T-shirts and had close-cropped hair. One of them came over to my table and looked down at me. 'I am a policeman,' he said.

I nodded.

'You have papers for Primorsko-Akhtarsk?'

'In my room,' I lied.

'Where have you come from?'

'Rostov-on-Don.'

'Rostov is the mother of crime –'

'– and Odessa is the father?'

He smiled, then glanced towards the bar and sat down. He whispered: 'I am not really a policeman.'

'What are you?'

'Special forces. OMON. But we are not allowed to talk about it.'

One of the others came over. He had a short fish-spine of stitches down his cheek. He locked his arm around the neck of the 'policeman', who winced. 'Fuck off, Oleg!'

Oleg laughed and pulled tighter. The policeman elbowed him in the stomach and Oleg let go. 'Ow!'

Oleg caught his breath and gestured to me: 'What's this?'

I told him.

'What do you want? This is our country.'

'Of course.'

'Our country! Russia!'

'Leave it, Oleg,' said the policeman.

But Oleg was already lunging at me. I fended him off. The policeman grabbed his arm and pulled him back. He tried again and the others at the bar came over and jostled him out.

'Come on, Oleg.'

Outside I could hear their shouting subside as they walked

down towards the beach. The policeman remained sitting opposite me.

'You have been in Chechnya?' he asked.

'No.'

He looked at me with bloodshot eyes. 'We're not supposed to talk about it, but I can tell you it's hell down there. You have your Ulster but this is twenty times worse. They come in and kill some of us and then they disappear. And the worst of it is this fucking blood feud. You kill one of theirs and they find you. I killed one a month or so back. Last week they found us at night on patrol and they got my friend. We had to bury him with our bare hands. They will find me when we go back, I am sure. They always fucking find us. We know they are coming and we can't do a damned thing about it.'

It was Sunday morning. The road out of Primorsko-Akhtarsk pushed south across a broad tableland of semi-reclaimed marsh. Drainage channels bordered the road and the water was hidden by beds of stooping reeds. The road was very straight but for the odd switch that sent it bucking over a wooden bridge, only to straighten out again on the opposite bank. In the distance the sky was a paler blue above the sea.

A woman in the hotel had put me on to her brother who was going fishing in the *liman*. He knew where to find the Old Believers. 'Them bearded fellows? 'course I know them.'

His mother had always said that her family had been Old Believers. But he only remembered his grandfather as a Cossack who wore his uniform on saints' days and never went outside in it. 'But all that's gone now, all destroyed!'

And now he was going fishing and worried only about the warden, who was armed, and his fellow poachers, who were also armed. 'I have only an old pistol and they have Kalashnikovs. What can I do? Last week they came in a boat and shot two fishermen.'

We reached the Old Believer village of Pokrovka and I waved him off towards the marshes. In the road was a herd of unattended cows, looking this way and that. Beyond them stood a large and newly-built church of yellow bricks. Women were spilling out of it in floral head-scarves and nineteenth-century dress. Skirting round the cows, I went to wait outside for the priest.

Father Gyorgi was a remarkable man. He had the greatness of those blessed with perfect historical timing. His ordination had coincided with the period of reforms, and he sensed the revived energies of the Pokrovka Old Believers bubbling up around him. He it was who had re-instigated the services and retaught the chants and who, without money, permission or expertise of any kind, had galvanised the community into building themselves a church. And this was no ordinary church. Lacking only a cupola or two, it was a fabulously ambitious structure that would have looked ornate even in a large town.

Opposite it stood an open-sided lean-to. There I sat out the heat of the afternoon with Father Gyorgi and a collection of the Pokrovka Old Believers. We arranged ourselves on benches at a long table and drank tea, while a mumble of bantams pecked in the dust. Beyond the flat fields was a line of reeds and beyond them was the sea.

Father Gyorgi wore a rimless cap of burgundy velvet. Shoulder-length hair fanned out beneath it. Quietly he invited each of the others to tell their stories or explain to me this point or that. Sometimes he himself would explain and sometimes, when others were talking, I would catch him looking away from us, one hand idly fingering his beard, his placid gaze fixed far off into the marshes.

The story of the Pokrovka Old Believers begins not long after the schism, in the first years of the eighteenth century. Peter the Great was driving Russia through one of its spells of frantic Westernisation. At six foot eight, Peter had two inches over Nikon and very different ideas of reform. He decreed Latin as the language of the seminary; and for his growing army of bureaucrats, German-tailored jackets. English, Italians and Catholics of all kinds poured into Russia with their fine crafts and opulent ways. From the provinces came renewed mutterings of the Antichrist and more than a dozen serious contenders to be the true tsar.

Peter had no time for Old Believers and banned beards completely. In the south, opposition grew, and in one Cossack uprising the *voeveda* himself only escaped the mob by hiding for three days in the village, long enough to grow a beard and pass for an Old Believer.

Bulavin was a Cossack from the south who also claimed to be the true tsar. He led a revolt against Peter in 1708 and when it failed, shot himself in the head. His main supporter was an ataman named Nekrasov. On Bulavin's death, Nekrasov led a flight of several thousand Cossacks and Old Believers out of Russia and into Ottoman Turkey.

In Turkey, the Old Believers spread out. Some remained in the hills of eastern Anatolia. Others reached Istanbul and became Bosphorus fishermen who forgot their language long before their Cossack ways and were recognised two hundred years later by White Cossacks fleeing the Bolsheviks. Another group of Old Believers pushed further round the Black Sea to the Danube delta. There they lived as the tide of the Ottoman empire ebbed south and all over *Mitteleuropa* the murmur of revolution filled the cafés. The Old Believers paid little heed. They received news of the Bolsheviks taking power in Russia with a certain ambivalence.

'It was a kind of paradise we had in Romania.' Father Gyorgi's mother was sitting beside her son. 'We would all come together to eat and say: should we have wine from this house or that house? We had everything we wanted. We lived in plenty from one year to the next. Our life was without trouble yet when the time came, we left for Russia without a second thought.'

After the Second World War, Stalin conducted a campaign to try to gather in some of the scattered Russian communities abroad. A colonel came and gave a lecture to the Old Believers about the life they would have in Russia, the cabins and schools and their own piece of land. Shortly afterwards a ship named *Karl Marx* came and took them to Odessa.

At the far end of the table, an elderly man stood up and said: 'I will tell you how it happened. When I got on that ship, first thing I did was take off my old boots and throw them in the sea. Far as I could. "Sergei," said my wife, "you're a fool. Why waste the shoes?" And I told her: "In Russia everyone wears new boots. You'll see."'

When the Old Believers reached Odessa, they waited on the quay. The lorries came after several days. They drove into the steppe to a new village with empty land all around it. It is yours, they were told, and the lorries left. But the village was nothing more than a few half-built concrete walls. The winter was one of the coldest on record. Many did not see out the first months. In the spring, those who survived made their way round by Rostov and down to Pokrovka.

The old man opened his arms. 'We'd come from the eighteenth century and were thrown into the twentieth. Is it any wonder that everyone took advantage of us and stole from us?'

Evening came upon Pokrovka with a barking of dogs and a slow lolloping of cows through the lanes. Moths flashed in and out of the roadside lamps. A pale yellow moon rose behind the

73

roofs of the village and Father Gyorgi said goodnight to his people and watched them as they left, one by one up the chalky track.

I asked him about the church, how it came to be built.

'It's a long story.'

'I'm in no hurry.'

We sat down again at the table. A chorus of frogs began from the marshes. Father Gyorgi paused, then leaned forward.

His account began in the time of Brezhnev. He was already studying to become a priest. Hunched over sketches in his kitchen, he and an architect friend talked about the problems of arches and apses and load-bearing walls. They drew up plans. It was a pointless exercise, he said. They were still locking up religious people. But in those days, you had to do something for yourself or you became dead inside.

Just as they finished the plans, Gorbachev came to power and made new laws about religion. At about this time Gyorgi was ordained and, feeling suddenly confident, thought he'd test the new laws out. He rolled up the plans and took them to the local authorities. But the local authorities said, 'Build a church? Whoever heard of such a thing!'

So he took the plans home and thought for a while. He sat at his table for some days and then decided: I will go to Moscow. He said goodbye to his wife and took a bus to the station. On the train he remembered something he'd been told by his architect friend: in Moscow, they never allow a scheme of any sort without asking for concessions. So, as the train sped north, he sketched in a few more cupolas and added another twenty feet to the length. That should do it, he thought.

At the ministry, he went in to see the official. 'I want to build a church in my village. I have brought the plans.'

The official said: 'Build a church? Why not?' He didn't even look at the plans.

Father Gyorgi was very pleased and returned to Primorsko-Akhtarsk to tell the authorities. They, in turn, were very angry.

'We must come and see the place,' they told him.

So the next day they drove out to see Father Gyorgi and the site. On the way, they were discussing ways to refuse the church when all at once their car turned over and landed in the ditch. Father Gyorgi went to visit them in the hospital and said: 'If you come again with such thoughts in your head, how can I be responsible for what happens to you?'

That was how he gained permission for the building of the church.

The construction itself was the next problem. No one in the village was a builder and no builder in the town had built churches. Father Gyorgi said: 'Let's just start and see what happens.'

He told them the first thing to do was to dig a hole for the foundations. When they had been digging for some weeks, people began to come past and say: 'How much longer are you going to carry on digging that hole, Father?'

And he would say to them: 'Not long now!'

But in truth he was worried. He knew if he didn't get the foundations right, he could never be sure of the church itself. So he called in an expert.

The expert looked at the work and shook his head and told Father Gyorgi that not even a bomb would damage such foundations. So Father Gyorgi told his men they must work a little longer. Then he called in the expert again and the expert said: 'Look, Father, why do you spend so much time? You could have done half the work and it would still be enough.'

So Father Gyorgi said to his men: we must work a little longer. When the expert came the third time, he said: 'What's the matter with you? You could build a cathedral on foundations like that!'

Father Gyorgi then said they were ready to start on the walls.

The walls presented their own difficulties. There was no stone in the area, so they decided to use brick. But there were no bricks either. Someone found some oven-bricks but the oven-bricks were hard to work, so they found a man in the Ukraine who had built his house with oven-bricks, but by then the man was old and when he had helped them build the walls up to the height of his shoulder, he sat down exhausted and said:

'I am seventy-two and at night I see two moons. You cannot expect me to climb a ladder.'

Father Gyorgi asked the Old Believers in the village to lay bricks. They said they couldn't do that. 'We're not qualified, Father. We wouldn't put them on straight.'

Father Gyorgi nodded thoughtfully. 'All right. If you don't get them straight first time, you just take them off and wipe them down and try again. It doesn't matter if you only lay five bricks in a day. That way you'll learn.'

'Very well, Father.'

'But remember,' he warned, 'they must be straight in the end because if they're not, in years to come your grandchildren will walk up and down this road and see the church, and if it's not right they will be ashamed and walk past in a hurry. But if it is right and the bricks are straight, they will stop and say to everyone: Look! It was my grandfather who helped to build that church.'

Father Gyorgi had to give the impression that he at least knew what was going on. But in truth he didn't have a clue. The others would come to him and say: 'Father, how do we do this bit?' And if it was easy, he would make something up, but if it was hard he would say: 'We're not quite ready to do that yet.' Then he'd go away and try to work it out.

After several months, everyone got the hang of it and Father Gyorgi was able to ask: 'What do you think is the best way to do this?' And they would discuss it and scratch their beards and say: 'Well, maybe if we did it this way . . . or like this . . .'

And sometimes when there was a very tricky bit, they would go off and pray, and when they'd all prayed for a while they would come back together and see what ideas they had, and if they had nothing they would agree that perhaps they had not prayed for long enough or in quite the right way. They would continue to pray until they had a solution. Sometimes it would take a week or more.

When it came to the cupolas on the inside of the church, they had a problem. They found it very difficult to make sure that the rim remained a true circle, and that as they built it up it remained centred on the square base. So they drilled a hole in one end of a plank, sharpened a tall pole and revolved the plank around the pole. When an architect came, he shook his head on seeing the device: 'That was the method the early Byzantine masons invented.'

The outside cupolas had to be made from metal and someone told Father Gyorgi of an Old Believer in Akhtarsk who worked in metal. He turned out to be just a watchmaker. But he said he'd help anyway. He had a friend in a shipyard and went and asked him about cupolas. 'Cupolas, hmm. Well, we would need to design and make a cast and a special alloy. Six months, three men – plus the design, that's five thousand dollars, maybe more.' The watchmaker cleared out his own garage and learned how to use a welding torch.

When he had completed the first cupola, he brought it in his car and put it on the grass and everyone agreed what a beautiful cupola it was. To get it up to the roof they put a block and tackle on the parapet and had a team up there and a team on the ground. They tied four knots on the cupola and then two more for safety. But halfway up the team on the roof started arguing with the team on the ground and suddenly all the knots untied and the cupola fell and broke into pieces. After that they were careful not to have any arguments.

When they started building, they had had about three hundred dollars in the bank, which lasted no time at all. Yet each time they had a bill to pay, money had a habit of turning up. Sometimes the old people would give their savings and sometimes suppliers would say: 'If it's for a church, you can have it for nothing.' Some money arrived anonymously. But gradually the costs went up, and towards the end Father Gyorgi spent most of his time raising funds from local businesses. With the last delivery of bricks, his luck ran out. He found that every one of his channels was exhausted. Although the bricks had already been used, the supplier was threatening to come and take them away again, even if it meant demolishing the church. There was much hard praying among the Old Believers.

Then, on the day the debt was due a man came to the village on the way to hunting in the *liman*. Seeing the scaffolding, he stopped and called out: 'What are you doing?'

'We are building a church!'

He stood there for a while watching them. Then he said, 'What a lot of pleasure you have given me.' And he turned round, went back to his home, and returned with the exact amount needed for the bricks.

They never saw that man again. They asked everyone they could think of who he was, but no one knew him. And although the man was a hunter and although he drove an old Moskvich, the rumour went round that he'd been an apparition of some sort, a saint or an archangel, or perhaps even Christ Himself.

Two of the elders of the village were standing by the church. They were fine old men with caps on their heads and chalky white beards. It was a crisp and dewy morning and I'd come back to look at the church.

'What do you think of our church?' asked one of the men.

'It's a beautiful church.'

'It's certainly beautiful.'

They started talking between themselves.

'You see, even foreigners know about the church now.'

'The whole world will come to know about it.'

'They say there'll probably be a thousand people at the opening ceremony.'

'A million, more likely.'

And they had stood like that for some time, these Old Believers who had been brought up on the far shores of the Black Sea, who had practised their faith in the name of a country they'd never seen, who were coaxed back to it with false promises and found it devoid of priests and churches – and they quietly acknowledged to each other that a little miracle had taken place in their village.

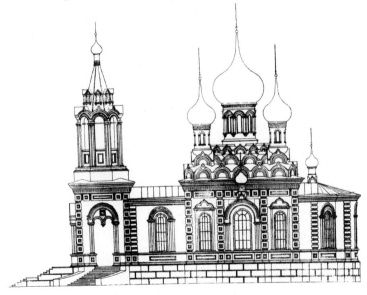

The Old Believer church at Pokrovka

The Coming of Allah and the KGB

The day or so planned for Pokrovka became a week. Each morning I woke in the attic room of Father Gyorgi's house, pulled back the curtain and looked out over the zinc roofs of the village to the meadows beyond. And each morning the canopy of the walnut tree was a little thicker, the sun a little higher and I told myself it was time to move on, to push south towards the mountains. At breakfast, Father Gyorgi would be there sitting with his youngest daughter on his knee telling me of such and such a man, or a widow or an old poet from the Romanian villages he'd been meaning to meet; or his friend Sasha was going fishing that day and would we help him – and each morning I raised my hand and said: 'All right, Father, you win. But tomorrow I leave.'

So we spent the days touring the communities around Pokrovka – sunlit mornings following levees across the salt lagoons, afternoons in crudely-daubed rooms, driving at dusk to see Old Believers in the remoter settlements, eating late at outside tables while each evening the moon grew a little bigger. And from Father Gyorgi I had the feeling that he too was uncovering things he'd never seen.

We sought out the Old Believers of the first settlement, those who had left the villages of the old Ottoman empire to live a carpet-bag existence during the years of war and revolution, who struggled up over the Caucasus and arrived here on the steppe to find no one but a few Cossacks breeding horses for the cavalry. Larisa Mikhailovna remembered seeing the flat land after the mountains, with nothing but grass taller than her head, and her mother parting the grass and pointing to a hole in the ground: 'There, my dear. Our new home.' Others spoke of famines and typhus and German tanks and a dark, airless church which made everyone faint. These ones had seen too the coming of the commissars who sent to the north all those who said they preferred their own beasts to the new tractors.

Those who'd survived it all lived now in adobe houses with carpets on the walls and bare boards on the floor. They sat on stools and on metal-framed beds and spoke with the weariness of a lifetime knowing that beyond their gate lay a world without kindness or reason. Being Old Believers had meant little to them but they clung to Father Gyorgi's hand and said: 'You're young, you're allowed to look at the past.'

They were grateful to him for coming, for being a priest, for teaching their grandchildren the old rites, for building the magnificent church as he had, and they followed him with their eyes as we left.

Then there were those like Father Gyorgi's own family who had come from Bulgaria and Romania after the war and had always observed the fasts; they had known nothing of the few years in the 1930s that had numbed the whole century. One old man, brought up on the old Danube delta, ended up in Daghestan and remembered arriving at the market. The Muslim traders, seeing his Old Believer beard, cried in fear: 'Allah! Allah! It is Allah come!'

Father Gyorgi knew well the effect his own unshorn beard created, and his unshorn hair and his black clerical robes. When we went into Primorsko-Akhtarsk, complete strangers would come up to him and say: 'Father, Father, I have this terrible anxiety . . .' or 'There's noises in my house, Father, like a ghost or something . . .' or 'Lost my little dog, Father, what's a good prayer to get him back?'

Some of them clearly irritated him, but in general he played the part and cocked his head and listened to their pleas and stressed that with faith you can do anything. He was a master at the theatricality that his supplicants required, and could call on the whole gamut of attitudes – gravely concerned, didactic, chiding, prophetically wise, through to dryly humorous or teasing.

One woman took him aside and while I listened to her husband complain about the Jews, she asked him what to do about their daughter who had taken up with a mafioso. On another occasion, on a hot afternoon we had stopped the car to cool off by a river. Father Gyorgi was in the shallows when a woman in a short white dress appeared on the bank, flicked back her hair and said: 'Baptise me, Father.'

Father Gyorgi had arranged that week for a painter to come and paint some angels. Inside the church it was cool and echoey. The painter was poised on a ladder with his chin pointed up at a partially-painted soffit. At the bottom of the ladder was a man named Sergei. Sergei was talking incessantly. Father Gyorgi took over from him, lodged his foot on the bottom rung and while he and the painter debated the exact iconography of the angels' wings, Sergei invited me to his home.

We walked out through the village on a sandy track. A thick ruff of grass ran down the middle. At the end of it was a cabin half-hidden by apple blossom. Sergei himself had built the cabin. His wife was beating a carpet and his two children were throwing water at each other. Beneath a willow was a fat, hobbled horse.

Sergei was a man of such radiant simplicity that I kept thinking I was sitting there with Dostoevsky's Prince Myshkin. Everything he said, every one of his gestures was propelled by a child's enthusiasm. Though he now wore the beard of an Old Believer, and though his peasant shirt was gathered at the waist with a woollen belt, he had been raised a Communist. 'The father of my mother was an Old Believer but she taught atheism in the school.'

He sat straight-backed on a wooden stool. His hands rested on his knees and while his face was constantly moving, sliding from one expression into the next, his body remained absolutely still. As a young man, he explained, his fidgetiness was unbearable. 'I always wanted to move house. I would say to my wife: "We must go and live in such and such a town because there our lives will be better!" But somehow it was always just the same.'

Ten years ago, having lived in the north and in Siberia and in the Urals, and in Kazakhstan, and on the edge of Moscow, Sergei and his family arrived in the town of Primorsko-Akhtarsk. There he heard about the community at Pokrovka and, remembering his grandfather had been an Old Believer, one day he said to his wife: 'I am going out for a walk.'

'I arrived in the village and there were men who looked like prophets. To tell you the truth, I was a little afraid because I knew the Old Believers were very strict. But they let me stand in their service. It was the Trinity and the church was full of yellow flowers and the Russian bell was ringing and when we came out of the church, the tables were full of food. It was like in a dream.

'The next Sunday I brought my family here and told them: "Look! It's where we're going to live." My wife said to me: "Sergei Ivanich, if we have to move once more, I will leave you." But then she saw the goodness of the people, and the tables full of food. Within a week we were all baptised and I knew I could stay here. I built the house and bought a horse.'

Sergei glanced at the horse who stood tail-swishing in the shadows. 'It was a very difficult life to start with. I put seeds in the ground and waited and waited. I'd never grown anything before. At night I'd go out and look at the ground where I'd put the seeds. For three weeks, nothing happened. I looked and looked at the ground – but nothing! Then one night the first shoot appeared and I woke my wife and she came out and looked. In those days I was working all the time and people kept coming past and saying: "Look, Seryozha, today's a feast day. Come and celebrate!" And I said, no, I have no time to celebrate.

'But then I noticed a strange thing. I became slower and slower. One day I couldn't move and as I lay there, I said to myself: Sergei, a life without holidays is like a horse with a bad owner!

'So now I celebrate all the feasts and when I'm working I get up at dawn, and work and eat, and afterwards I come and lie down underneath the tree with a glass of water and I am completely satisfied.'

Before going to church, Sergei explained how he would call on those in the community whom he thought he might have offended. He would ask their forgiveness. Often he would go into someone's house and apologise and they would say: 'Sergei, we don't know what you're on about. We didn't even notice what you'd done.' And he visited the other houses too, just in case he'd offended them without knowing it. It all took a very long time but he didn't mind because he loved to talk and he was able to go to church happy.

'It's difficult in those services because they're so long. They go on and on, for hours! You stand and stand and you can hardly go on standing. But then afterwards you come home and you feel not just clean in your soul but in your body as well and you're all dressed up and your wife looks beautiful and everything else looks beautiful too.'

Sergei haltered his horse and rode beside me as I walked back to the village. At the church he left me and I watched him set off towards the *liman*, his horse slow and broad-rumped, Sergei himself already lost in thought.

Father Gyorgi had heard of another priest, an icon-painter who lived in a leafy stanitsa some way inland from Pokrovka. Father Yevgeny had a great reputation.

'He is a master. He paints in the old way.' Father Gyorgi's tone was reverential, though he'd never met the man.

We found Father Yevgeny in a warehouse the Cossacks had requisitioned for purposes that were not entirely clear. Through chinks in the roof came a bright rigging of sunshafts which fell on the earthen floor and on piles and piles of military crates.

Father Yevgeny worked in a room at one end of the warehouse. He was not an Old Believer, but said that those distinctions counted for nothing now, in the wake of an atheistic era. 'We are faced with an empty steppe. Why build two fences when together we could build one twice as quickly?' And when he spoke of the imperative of technique in his icons, it was with exactly the same conviction as Old Believers talked of the old rites.

He was a few years older than Father Gyorgi. His beard already 'showed the frost in it'. He had the dazed intensity of someone who has stared at the same thing for a very long time.

For me, icons themselves have never been as interesting as the passions they produce in others. To Father Yevgeny, as to the first Byzantine painters, they are the closest the material world could come to God. The Doukhobors, on the other hand, see them as worthless lumps of iron and wood. In the monastic towns of Yaroslavl and Kostroma, monks used to take those too dark to restore down to the Volga and, with appropriate prayers, consign them to its waters. There they drifted down through the forests to the plains where the Tatars plucked them out and ate horse-steaks off them, saying: 'What kind of god is this, which is no better than a gridiron?' Converts to the Five-Year Plan, who saw the Church as 'the kulaks' agitprop', ripped the icons from the church walls and scattered them on the floors of the kolkhoz piggeries.

More than a millennium earlier, Leo III of Byzantium had also taken violently against icons, and ordered the destruction of every one. Their return to favour a century and a half later marked the beginning of the great age of icons. The belief grew that painting gave form to the spirit in the same way that God made Himself flesh in Christ. Icons became the visual word, and purists regarded as heresy the development of less stylised painting in the West, where the restless knaves of the Renaissance were overturning Byzantium's stiff abstractions.

Father Yevgeny leaned towards me. 'Today in Russia they have lost sight of the real icons. I have even seen them hanging in our churches paintings by Raphael!'

In the middle of his studio, lying flat on several trestles was a large, half-completed icon. It showed Christ Acheiropoietos, the Face of the Saviour 'not made with hands'. This was the first of all icons, the one which most literally reveals the incarnate properties of painting. Made, it is said, when Christ Himself pressed His face to a veil, the first version was sent to King Agbar of Edessa, whose leprosy was instantly cured by looking into it. And it was this icon whose triumphant entry into Constantinople in 944 heralded the return to grace of the banished images.

Father Yevgeny spread his arms over it. The outline of the face had been drawn in and some of the gilding applied; elsewhere was just a base of deep red. I asked him about his technique and he led me to a corner where a stack of untreated boards lay awaiting preparation. He spoke with absolute precision, as if explaining a spell.

The wood he used was lime when he could get it and pine when he could not (in Byzantium it had been lime and cypress). Having fashioned the boards, he placed linen across them and on the linen a layer of fish glue.

'It must be fish glue.'

He then applied a gesso surface of ground clay and egg yolk which as it dried caused the linen to shrink and bind the boards tight.

'The egg must be fresh that day.'

The pigments he made from lumps of raw malachite and lapis, and an extract of sulphur. First the rocks were pummelled with a pestle and mortar, then the dust was taken and with a pig of iron ground even finer against a slab of polished granite.

'It must be granite.'

A base of red clay went on first, tempered with egg white and beeswax. Onto this were laid the pigments, and then the gilding which was the most delicate and hallowed of all the stages – the intercession of the process. Taking a book of gold leaf and a blade, Father Yevgeny cut out a page and placed it on a cushion of brown suede. 'It must be the thinnest of blades to cut the gold.' Rubbing the back of his hand with a little sunflower oil ('It must be sunflower oil') he took a brush and wiped it once, gently, over the oil. With the bristles primed he was able to pick up the gold leaf and, cupping it with his other hand, cross the room to the work. Before putting the gold in place, he poured a few drops of vodka on the base.

I said: 'It must be Russian vodka, I suppose.'

He looked at me without smiling. 'Of course.'

He placed the sliver of gold in exactly the right place on Christ's halo. 'All the light in an icon must come out of the saint himself.' He removed the brush and took a piece of unspun cotton to wipe it down. Once it was flat he burnished the gold with a lump of polished agate mounted on a stick of pine.

Father Yevgeny straightened his back. In the failing light he crossed the room and pointed to a place on another icon where he had used a lapis pigment for the folds of the Virgin's robe. 'These colours will stay for ever. If you go to the old icons you will see that the paints have changed back into the rocks themselves. I knew a blind woman who could run her fingers over the iconostasis and know exactly which saints they were, and what were the colours, just from the different feel of the pigments.'

I asked him what it was that had first made him paint. When after a pause he spoke, he was suddenly free of all the dogma and I warmed to him for the first time.

'When I was a child I used to stand in front of icons in the services. I did not understand the chants and the readings but I could see the way that light was held inside the icons. I felt at the same time a light in me, an ecstasy, and ever since I have felt the same ecstasy in the face of beauty – not just joy but an ecstasy so intense I do not know what to do. That is what makes me paint. Every artist must have this sense of ecstasy in them. It is like a light burning inside you and you must capture and share it with others.'

When we left Father Yevgeny's studio, it was already dusk. We drove back to Pokrovka between wheat fields and drainage channels whose waters shone in the late sun. By the time we reached Pokrovka the stars were bright against a clear sky.

Sasha's steel-hulled craft skated across the *liman*. He was crouching in the stern with the helm cradled under his arm. Terns dipped and hovered over the churned-up water astern. Father Gyorgi was sitting barefoot on the narrow foredeck, and the strands of his beard and his hair trailed behind him. We were going crayfishing.

Sasha was a youngish Old Believer who was also a fisherman and he had laid some pots in one of the far lagoons. His outboard produced more noise than power. For a long time the strip of reeds on the horizon grew no wider. When after an hour or so we were upon it Sasha closed the throttle and the bows slumped down and the stern wave sluiced past us. We followed the line of reeds until there was a gap; turning into it, Sasha eased open the throttle again.

Among the reeds was a vast labyrinth of canals. Some were wide enough for a ship, others so narrow you could put out your hand on either side and flick the reed-stalks as they passed. There were the husks of lotus flowers in the water, and turtles, and a kingfisher which raced jewel-backed ahead of us, and herons which flew out from the reeds with their slow-motion flight. At one point a few feet of steel plate stuck out of the water and Sasha leaned forward and over the noise of the engine told me the story of a MiG which had ditched there a few years ago; its Ethiopian trainee pilot ejected into the swamp and when he came out of the water and took off his helmet the fishermen had run away in terror.

The canals opened out into another lagoon which was ringed only by the slimmest, most distant ring of reeds.

Sasha had not buoyed his nets. Either bandits or the law would steal them if he had. He cut the engine and aligned the landmarks and we trailed a kedge until the line was hooked. One by one the small creels dropped in over the side. The translucent backs of the crayfish squirmed on the bottom-boards in a flexing, chitinous mass. When all the nets were in, we idled into the shore until the bows bumped and rode up the bank. Sasha pulled up the outboard.

The wind was blowing through the reeds and the old stalks

clicked like bones. There was nothing around us for miles but water and reed-beds and canals and swamp. Sasha bent down and pushed the pile of crayfish forward; he retrieved a bottle of vodka from the bilges. I took out a knife and cut the bread while Father Gyorgi unpeeled a lump of pig fat from its grease-proof paper. We had tomatoes and spring onions and a few potatoes. Father Gyorgi crossed himself while Sasha laid out three beakers on the gunwale, and filled them with vodka. Handing them to us, he addressed Father Gyorgi with the question which had clearly been troubling him for some time:

'What's all this about Jesus being a Jew, Father?'

'He was a Jew, yes.'

'So how come we're Christian and the Jews are Jewish?'

'The Jews didn't think Jesus was the Messiah.'

'But before the Jews became Jews, they were Russians, right? I mean, wasn't everyone Russian, at the beginning?'

'Not exactly –'

'Who were they?'

'African.'

'African!' Sasha laughed at that and shook his head and I could see he thought Father Gyorgi was out of his depth on that one. 'OK, Father. What about this? I heard that a *banya*'s not allowed on a feast day. Can it be so wrong to wash?'

'Of course you can wash, just not in the *banya*.'

And so it went on. Father Gyorgi addressed each of Sasha's points with unswerving logic.

'So, why shouldn't we eat meat on Wednesday or Friday? I mean, why those days particularly?'

'No reason. It could equally well be Monday or Tuesday.'

'It just seems they're having us on a lot of the time with these rules. Half of them don't make any sense.'

Father Gyorgi shifted his position against the spray-screen. 'It's not the rules that are important, Sasha, but the obeying of them. These rules are a way of practising discipline. If you can keep up with the small rules then when bigger questions come it will be easier to make the right choice. Without obedience to a set of rules our lives would have no value. A man cannot survive without some set of rules. Of course you won't get ill if you eat meat on a fast day. But by not eating meat, you are showing to yourself that you have control, that you can live by rules. For instance, this belt we wear' – Father Gyorgi pointed to the woven belt worn outside his shirt in the old *muzhik* style – 'it is worn as a symbol of submission, showing obedience to the law, like a vow. Married women wear a knotted headscarf for the same reason. In the old days, criminals were made to walk around without a belt. They had a word meaning "unbelted" which meant you were banished by the law.'

Sasha nodded and continued his questioning and Father Gyorgi continued his instruction until a cool wind came up from the south. We pushed the boat back into the water and hid the crayfish but we met no patrols and reached the berth shortly after dark.

That was the last evening with the Old Believers. We ate at Sasha's, seven of us sharing the crayfish from a great vat. A basin was put out for the shells and when the vat was empty and the basin full, a man named Stefan started talking about his arrival in Russia after the war.

'To tell the truth, I was surprised. I'd been raised on stories of the tsar and a picture book we had of St Petersburg.' Stefan was thus a little disappointed to find himself living in a southern swamp. He told a long story about an officer who came to see him in the early days. The officer had seemed a nice enough man and was very interested in Stefan's life in Bulgaria, so they chatted away about that until the officer asked about the others who'd come. Stefan raised his hand and told him that no, he could not talk for others – the officer would have to ask them himself. As he left, the officer told Stefan he'd call again in a few weeks.

'At the time, I was a little bit worried. I thought I'd better not tell my wife. But she sensed it anyway. And the strange thing was that when I told her what was worrying me, I seemed to forget about it and carried on with my normal life.'

But the officer came back and asked Stefan what he had. Stefan said: 'What do you mean?' Then the officer's men started beating him and when they stopped, they said: 'The next time we will not spare you.' After that he was very worried because he knew he could not speak for his friends and he did not want to die.

'But me and the wife had a little talk. After a bit we forgot all about it and we carried on with our normal life.'

When the officer came again, it was the middle of the night. They pulled Stefan from the bedroom. He said he still couldn't talk about his friends and the officer shouted at him: 'Scum! You have three days and then you will hang!'

At that, Stefan became extremely worried. His wife was worried too. She didn't get out of bed. When the third day came, Stefan sat by the door muttering the old prayers. He sat there all day. In the evening he looked through the curtains but still there was no sign of the officer. The next day there was no sign either, nor that whole week, nor at all that month, and pretty soon his wife was up and after they'd had a bit of a talk, somehow they forgot all about it and carried on with their normal life.

'I never saw that man again. He just vanished from this earth!'

Beside Stefan was another Old Believer, a giant of a man named Igor. Igor had served in the Bulgarian navy and of all the days he served, the one that stood out for him most was the day they raced the English sailors.

'We only had two ships in our navy, but one day one of them English ships came into Varna. White ship, it was. What a ship!'

The ship anchored some way out and put out a tender which was rowed over to the Bulgarians. A group of English sailors shipped their oars and an officer stood up in the stern: 'Ahoy there! We'd like to challenge you to a race.'

'Well, we leaned over the side and looked down at these English sailors in their polished-up boat with their little white hands like ladies' hands, and we thought, yes, we'll have a race. We had great big hands with blisters all over and our tender was all oily and rusty. But we said, we will race you, of course.'

'And who won?'

'We did! They were fifty metres behind us at the end. They asked us on their ship afterwards and our boots made marks on their decks. I remember we had a few bottles with us and they gave us pieces of cake. I don't think I'll ever see another ship like that. Not as long as I live.'

The next morning, with the walnut leaves now fully unfurled, I told Father Gyorgi that it really was time to leave and he said: 'Of course. Just one more thing. I want you to meet Grigory.'

Grigory was head of the local television channel. I agreed to do an interview for him. The questions didn't stray very far from the price of butter in Britain and what they cooked there for their evening meal. And although I was trying to maintain a low profile, to keep away from the view of the authorities, and although appearing on television was a fairly foolish way to go about it, it all seemed harmless enough.

I said goodbye to Father Gyorgi at the TV station, marvelling for the last time at the way he juggled his roles, how he could stand there, amidst the electronics in a sound-mixing studio, looking for all the world like a nineteenth-century *starets*.

A few days later, from another town, I telephoned him. He told me that after the interview had been broadcast, Grigory received a visit from the FSB, the KGB's post-Soviet entity. Who was this Englishman? they demanded. What was he doing in this town?

'What did Grigory say?' I asked, with some apprehension.

'He said: "If you were doing your job properly, then you'd know"! And he added that unfortunately the Englishman has left the region. And no, he had no idea where to.'

Solzhenitsyn and the Trousers of Prince Vaja

I had a friend in Moscow who was researching the early life of Solzhenitsyn and she'd told me about an old estate that had once belonged to the writer's grandfather. All she knew about it was that it was in a village called Otrado-Kubanskoe, that the village was near Armavir and that it was now, of all things, an institute of bee-keeping.

I reached Armavir a day after leaving Father Gyorgi. It was a hot afternoon. I wandered down through the town to the river – the river Kuban. I sat on the bank and watched a woman in a swimsuit ride in and out of the water on a young gelding. She rode the horse bareback and held him tightly-reined as they splashed through the shallows. The river was swift from the mountains and when I swam into the main channel it swept me a hundred yards downstream before I touched bottom again. I walked back and lay on the grass. The woman and the horse stopped their splashing. They kicked up the bank and rode out into the steppe. In the distance was the hum of Armavir. A plane droned across the empty sky. I fell asleep.

Beyond Armavir, the Kuban cuts through a platform of black-earth steppe. In the years before the Revolution, a group of pioneers had settled here along the new railway and parcelled out the land. They had grown fat on its yields. They experimented with crop rotations and cattle breeds. They reared silky-flanked horses and built houses which dazzled the peasants with their opulence. Zakhar Shcherbak was one of these men. He had started as a shepherd boy in the Ukraine but by 1914 had amassed a total of twenty thousand sheep. His son drove one of only nine Rolls-Royces in Russia. His grandson is Aleksandr Solzhenitsyn.

The next morning I took a train to Otrado-Kubanskoe. The station was nothing more than a low shed. No one else got off. I crossed the rails and asked a woman about the institute.

'Eh?'

'Is there a bee institute near here?'

'A what institute?'

'Bees.'

'There's no bees here.'

'What about an institute?'

'No institute.'

'Nothing nearby?'

'Look, there's no bees and there's no institute!'

She was sitting on a bench and she turned to look up the road. Her dress was patterned with sunflowers. 'Unless it's that botanical institute you're on about.'

The day was hot. The wind blew in from the steppe and the crops swayed and nodded before it. Larks sang unseen in a sky which was criss-crossed with high cloud. After some time I heard a car behind me. A man wound down his window, a man with wild-looking hair and a single tooth in his mouth like a mattock blade. I told him I was looking for a big old house at the botanical institute. 'Do you know it?'

'I know it. Get in.'

A pig's head sat beside him on the front seat. I climbed into the back.

'This house of yours,' he said into his mirror. 'What's it to you? You want to buy it?'

'A family called Shcherbak lived there.'

'There's no one by that name.'

'It was a long time ago.'

'A long time ago, eh?'

'Before the Revolution.'

'Well, you'll have to ask the old people about that.'

The old people lived in the cottages near the institute. They were very keen to help: Oh yes, there'd been a house here. Before the Revolution, yes, it was built then. A very big house – the biggest! Shcherbak, yes, that was the name of the family.

I asked if the house still stood.

Of course! But no one could tell me quite where it was, and it became clear they'd been saying 'yes' because they could see how much it pleased me when they said 'yes' and they knew that if they said 'no' I'd be disappointed, and I'd come such a long way.

I walked back down the road to the institute office where a man named Gravchenko confirmed what I'd assumed: there was no pre-Revolutionary house, and no family called Shcherbak.

Gravchenko was on his way to lunch. He wore a Kirghiz hat with a stiff brim. He had a wide-open face and an easy smile and we walked briskly to the canteen. We ate a meal of meat and potato and drank water. Then Gravchenko began to talk.

He'd been born in Belorussia, one of seven children. In 1941 he'd travelled to Leningrad to help save the city from the Wehrmacht. As autumn closed in so did the Germans, cutting off the supply routes one by one.

'We ate dogs and birds and when there were none left we boiled the boots of the dead men to make soup. We stacked up the frozen bodies as if they were logs. But you wouldn't understand about that.'

His wrist was scarred from the time a sniper caught him as he foraged around the lines; he'd been wounded in the chest.

The siege lasted two and a half years – nine hundred days – and left half the city dead. Gravchenko returned to his village in the summer of 1944. The forest and the fields were dotted with blue flowers and yellow flowers. The road was a pale strip between pine forests. It was just as he remembered it.

'That was the moment I was filled with all the happiness of my boy years.'

The area had suffered badly during the occupation and he reached his house to find a family from Lida living there. Of his own family, not one had survived. The partisans had been active in the area, and the Germans had put the Gravchenko family in a barn and burned them all. In his house, Gravchenko recovered a book of fairy tales that had once belonged to his youngest sister. With that under his arm, he left Belorussia for ever. He spent ten years in Kazakhstan, then in a closed nuclear city in Siberia. He'd won a competition to work at the botanical institute and it was a good job. He'd never married and had only colleagues, not friends. Gravchenko was in a way the model Soviet citizen: the *blokadnik*, the orphan, loyal to nothing except the state, which was the one thing that had never let him down.

He asked me why the Shcherbak house interested me so much.

'Oh yes,' he said. 'The Solzhenitsyn house.'

'You know it?'

He nodded. 'It's not here. It's Novokubansk you want.'

So I left Gravchenko and the botanical institute and hitched a lift back up the valley. I left the main road on foot.

The Shcherbak house and its buildings had spawned a village, and the village had grown into a small town which served the Centre for Experimental Farm Machinery. Odd devices lay everywhere – elaborate seed-drills, a novel hay-roller, a kind of split-level harrow, ploughs that looked like outsize kitchen utensils. The municipal railings had a motif of tractors running through them.

It was not difficult to find the house itself. It stood amidst a thick balsam-smelling copse. The traces of a vast array of outbuildings were all around – stables, grain-stores, icehouses, long low byres for the cattle and long low barracks for the labourers. The trees and lilac bushes had all outgrown themselves and the house, with its broad eaves and high windows, was empty and unused.

In *August 1914*, Solzhenitsyn writes of the estate – the five and a half thousand acres of black Kuban earth. And he writes of his grandfather who'd built it – his gold cigarette case and Havana cigars, the plans he drew up with an architect. He writes of the million ironstone bricks it took to build the house, the jalousies and venetian blinds to keep out the summer heat, the lemon-tree tubs brought in for the winter, the lawns of English rye-grass kept trim by motor-mowers, the lake of a swimming pool, the electric lanterns in the park. Solzhenitsyn did not write of the small building set apart from the house where Shcherbak, who never quite shook off his shepherd-boy past, actually chose to live.

After the Revolution, Zakhar Shcherbak went south to Kislovodsk for safety. There he saw the Reds and Whites come and go. Somehow he survived the accompanying slaughters. In time though, when it all settled down, he was drawn back to the Kuban. To avoid arrest he lived anonymously in a neighbouring village. He learnt to depend on the charity of his former employees, and year by year he witnessed the slow crumbling of his achievement.

A woman was walking her dog in the park. She said she always walked her dog there because she loved the house. Her eyes were soft and her hands delicate; the dog was a Doberman pinscher. She had been very excited last year because Solzhenitsyn himself had come to see the house.

'It was the happiest day of my life! He looked at the house, then spoke to the crowd for a long time. Such a great man! I have all his photographs and newspapers in an album.'

She said she couldn't quite remember what he'd said. But she loved his books. She had the complete set, a long row of matching editions, locked up with the albums in a glass-fronted cupboard in her flat, free from dust and any of those other blemishes that might come from turning the pages.

Her husband was a government official. He spent the evening in silence while his wife talked of books and asked me questions about Britain. In the end he raised his hand and stopped her mid-sentence. He then rose and placed before me, in ascending order of size, a large collection of guns. 'We have only daughters,' he said.

He was going hunting that weekend. In the morning he asked me to go with him. But I had to be back in Armavir to meet a Molokan.

It had been a messy kind of an afternoon – one of those afternoons trying to get things done in Russia that leaves you thinking things really aren't meant to get done, that effort of any sort is a strange and subversive activity. I had trawled Armavir and had not found the member of the Molokan sect. I had found a man named Sasha who said he knew the Molokans and we were sitting in the outer hallway of a communal flat in an old merchant's house. It was dark in the hall and everything was dusty and old. I was on the phone when the outside door opened and in walked a man wearing the uniform of the Kuban Cossacks. He was in an expansive mood.

'What? Out in the passage? Come on in.'

He was a thin, elderly man with the eyes of a ten-year-old boy. He had come to see his niece, and he showed us in to her high-ceilinged room for a minute or two. I should have known better.

The table filled at once with bottles and plates of meat and cheese, and with each plate and each bottle the tight control I was trying to keep on my plans slackened. I resigned myself to it. I went out to the kiosk and added some champagne and vodka to the table. When I let on that it was my birthday, I knew there was no turning back.

The Cossack's niece was Anechka. She was married to a man named Vaja who was Georgian. A Georgian prince, said the Cossack. (It has to be said that they are not rare, these Georgian princes. As with everything else that was good in life, titles were dished out generously by the Georgians, and by the nineteenth century there were thousands of them.)

Prince Vaja stood and stretched out his arm. 'I would like to drink first to my Cossack uncle for bringing these friends . . . and to the birthday of Philip our friend from England which is such a long way away in France.' He threw back his glass and let out a hiss of satisfaction. Anechka tugged at his shirt, trying to get him to sit down; instead he crossed the room and took a picture from the wall. It was a map of Georgia.

'Look.' He placed it before me. 'This is the country of my birth. You like it?'

'Yes.'

'Have it!'

'No, Vaja. It's your country.'

'Yes, and it's your birthday!'

'You need it more than me.'

'Have you ever been to Georgia?' he asked.

'Once. I'm on my way there now.'

'Oh – oh, I love my country,' he pressed the map to his chest, 'and I miss it with all my heart. Take it!'

'You're in Russia now. You need it.'

'But I love Russia too. And I love my wife. She is Russian. In the time of the union, everything was easy and we used to travel there and there were no borders. Russia and Georgia were one –'

At that moment the door opened and, tossing Georgia onto his bed, Vaja greeted the man who entered. 'Sergei!'

Sergei also lived in the flat and for years had run, from the communal kitchen, a *samizdat* newspaper; in the seventies he had served his time as a political prisoner. He was a vast man, completely bald, who moved with a certain bird-like grace.

Vaja poured more drinks, and stood again. He placed his hand on Sergei's bulky shoulder. 'This man – this man is an honest man and a good man. Always fighting for what's right. I respect him like a brother, like a father. We've been neighbours for many years and I respect him so much. In fact, he probably doesn't even know how much I respect him.'

The Cossack nodded: 'A brave man!'

'Really a fighter for truth.'

'A hero!'

Sergei cocked his head. 'What's the point of such words? I mean, where do they lead us?'

Vaja ignored him. 'Without such men we would be beset by badness! To do good always, it's all we can hope to achieve in this life. I myself am always trying to do good. And my wife too. Today she bought me a pair of trousers. When you come back home and your wife has bought you a pair of trousers, well . . .' He turned to her and kissed the top of her head.

'Come on, Vaja, show your new trousers,' urged the Cossack.

Vaja went into a cupboard to look for them. There was a yelp of discovery. But instead of his trousers, he returned with a three-volume biography of Marshal Zhukov. He put it on the table in front of me. 'Here, Philip. For your birthday!'

'No, Vaja.'

'I queued for three days to get this book.'

'Well, you must keep it.'

'No, it's brand new, I promise you. I haven't read a single word.'

The Cossack leaned over the table towards Sergei. 'You know about politics.'

'I have opinions.'

'Tell me this, then. Where did they come from?'

'Who?'

'These idiots who are our politicians.'

'What do you mean, "Where did they come from?" We voted for them.'

'I didn't vote for them.'

'Others did.'

'Well, they must be crazy!'

'It's democracy.'

'They're bandits, the lot of them. We should get rid of them like –'

'Quiet!' Vaja jumped up again. 'Cackling like a lot of old women.'

He started another speech. 'We whose hearts are always open and whose tables are always full of strangers –'

Sergei waved an upturned palm at him. 'So Georgians are hospitable?'

'The most hospitable people in the world!'

'Why do you have all these wars then?'

Vaja paused for a moment. 'I don't know. Georgia is being punished for its hospitality. We are being robbed and looted. If someone came to this door tomorrow and said: "Vaja, you must come and fight for your country," I would not look behind me for one second.'

'Would it be worth dying for?'

'Of course! They could kill me. They could crucify me! They could put nails here . . . and here. We welcome all other people in our country – Ossetians, Armenians, Abkhaz – and then they want to be separate. Why? I do not understand it. It's as if I ask you into my house and you stay one day, and I say you're welcome! Then you stay two days, and I say you're welcome! After three, four days the same – and on the fifth day you turn to me and say: "Get out, Vaja!" It is like being told to leave my own house.'

Several minutes passed as he explained the wars in Georgia, and how the Georgians wanted only friendship and how these people just came in and cut bits off his country as if it were a dead sheep. His voice became more plaintive, his tone more disbelieving. Then he faltered.

The Cossack looked up at him: 'Well?'

'So much has gone now –'

'But what is it we're drinking to?'

'Wait, wait . . .'

The glass continued to wave undrunk in one hand, a cigarette unlit in the other. He looked above our heads. 'What will become of you, Georgia, when surrounded by such people? When you offer your hand in friendship and you get a gun in return –'

'Vaja,' hissed Anechka.

'– when you offer help and they spit in your face. And old people are driven from their homes with nowhere to go. Nowhere. I would lay down my life for them if only it would help. I would give every rouble I own and sell my clothes and my television if I could help those people fight back for what is theirs. Right now I'm going to –'

'Vaja.' Anechka placed her hand on his arm.

'I will –' He looked down into his glass. 'I'm sorry. Perhaps it would be better . . .' He went again to the cupboard and reappeared buttoning up a pair of khaki trousers. 'My new trousers.'

He pulled in the belt and looked down at his new trousers

and then looked at his wife. He took up his glass and drank it down. 'I'm sorry.'

He left the room. After he'd gone, the conversation was hesitant. Then it started up and before long was as lively as before. From time to time I looked to the open door and saw Vaja sitting in the hall, chin cupped in his hands, staring at the floor. And even later, when another debate had begun – about the failure of dissidents and the disappointment of Solzhenitsyn's return, about the re-emergence of the Communists – and long after that when it had drifted on into its looser phases, when everything was repetitive and unconnected, I could see Vaja in the same position in the hall, staring at the floor, his princely elbows propped on the knees of his brand new trousers.

The Death of Kuzma Alekseyevich

After another day's looking, I found the Molokan. He was a pale and silent man and he gave me an address in Kochubeyevskoe.

I took a train and a bus, and another bus, and in the late afternoon I arrived on the town's leafy fringes. A hot wind was blowing in from the steppe, and with it came a thick haze of dust which dried the mouth and stuck to the teeth. In the haze hung the crimson ball of the sun. On the far side of town, I pushed open a door in a high fence. A concrete yard lay behind it; a well, a walnut tree and a collection of single-storey buildings. In the middle of the yard stood a white-bearded man in a felt hat.

'Timofei Vassiliyevich?'

'It is me.'

I had reached the chief Molokan of all Russia.

My trail to the Molokan sect, the 'milk-drinkers', had begun four years earlier, in a town in the Armenian highlands. Amidst the swarthy market crowd of Dilijan was a group of blonde-haired, high-cheeked women selling tomatoes. 'Molokans,' they said. 'We're Molokans from the Tambov region and we were sent here.'

'When?'

'Hundred and fifty years ago, by Tsar Nicholas I.'

They sketched out the beliefs that had led to their exile – the violent reaction against the priesthood, the store they set by the dietary laws of Leviticus, the close identification they felt with the early Christian communities. We talked for some time and I left the town feeling buoyed up by their zest, their furtive commitment, and by the blood-red tomatoes with which they filled my pockets.

A year later, spine-reading in a second-hand bookshop in Somerset, I came across a book called *The Pilgrims of Russian Town: The Community of Spiritual Christian Jumpers in America*. The shelves of the bookshop were stocked with hunting memoirs, stag lore, yellow-paged thrillers, but this book stood out among them with the sparkling incongruity of the women in the Dilijan market. On the book's frontispiece was a Tolstoyan figure, hat in hand, captioned 'An elder of the Spiritual Christians'. The chapters which followed were entitled 'Molokan Tradition', 'The Molokan Family', 'The Struggle to Perpetuate Molokanism'. The Spiritual Christian Jumpers were the Molokans. I bought the book for a fiver.

All sorts of theories have been put forward to explain why the Molokans, or 'milk-drinkers', are so named. Their own is the most convincing. They point to a passage in the First Epistle General of Peter:

> As newborn babes, desire the sincere milk of the word, that ye may grow thereby . . .

For Molokans, nothing but the word is worthy of veneration – not icons nor priests, not bricks and mortar, not the Cross, not the Virgin nor long-limbed saints. Only through the word comes the pure milk of the Holy Spirit, and this alone is the manifestation of God. Like the Gnostics, the Molokans recognise that some and not all of their number are destined to receive the spirit, and in doing so these elect Molokans become 'little Christs'. It is to them that, in the *sobraniye*, the deepest bows are directed.

Although the Molokans grew from a similar root to the Doukhobors, they dismiss that version of textless devotion. And in terms of numbers, the Molokans were more successful. During the nineteenth century they became a rallying-point for dissenting Russians and their numbers swelled to more than a million. One branch in the 1820s, under the teachings of a peasant named Popov, pooled their possessions and their resources and coined the term 'Communists' for the first time. Another branch in 1833 experienced 'a great outpouring of the Holy Spirit' and took to joyous leaping in recognition of it. They became known as *Priguny*, or 'jumpers'.

In 1865 a booklet was published in Geneva entitled *The Confession of Faith of the Spiritual Christians called Molokanye*. Written by members of the sect themselves, it traces their origins to the reign of Ivan the Terrible. Moscow at that time was a hive of fear, xenophobia and millenarian superstition. There was an English physician at court whose very foreignness was, by all accounts, a terrifying thing to behold. Muscovites rushed to bar their doors whenever they saw him, and many considered him to be the Antichrist. One merchant however, coming as he did from Tambov – that town of dissenters – approached the doctor and during their long discussions learnt from him something that was then largely unknown to the Russian laity: the Bible.

On his return home, the Tambov merchant relayed the secrets to a landowner, Matvei Semyonovich Bashkin, who at once saw the evil of a Church which obscured from its people the word of God. Henceforth Bashkin led his life according to the less ambiguous aspects of Christ's teaching. He followed only the rules pronounced in the Sermon on the Mount, freed his serfs, dared to teach the Gospels, and although he was arrested for his subversive ways, and was tortured and broken on the rack, his revelations took root in Tambov's fertile soil and two hundred years later bloomed in the form of the Molokan sect.

Like the Doukhobors, the Molokans were an intolerable threat to the orthodoxy of Church and state, who dealt with them in the usual fashion – by banishing them to the empire's emptier regions. Some were despatched in chains across the ice to the far north. Beside them rode a priest in a sledge; all they had to do was to kiss his pectoral cross and they were free. Others were forced south, to the hot and hostile regions of the Transcaucasus – Armenia, Georgia and, for the group of Timofei's ancestors, Azerbaijan. Here they lived in isolated communities and avoided too much contact with the alien peoples around them. And like the Doukhobors in the same area, they had learnt of late that independence was synonymous with chauvinism and war. They had moved north again, back into Russia.

That first evening with the Molokans we all ate outside at a long table. The walnut tree spread its pale green canopy over our heads. Timofei Vassiliyevich sat at one end, high-chinned and patriarchal. His wife and his three sons, and their three wives and their older children were ranked along the table before him. Beside him, disciple-like, sat a man named Mikhail.

I asked Timofei what had made them leave Azerbaijan and he leaned back on his stool and a silence fell around the table. The shadows shifted beneath his brow. 'It was the year 1987 and we were living in Sumgait.'

Mikhail continued: 'One night a voice came to him in a dream and told him to take his people.'

'It was the word of God.'

'So you left at once?'

'We left.' Timofei paused. 'The pogroms started as soon as we were gone. We travelled through the hard mountains. We had with us our belongings and when we reached this place we decided to settle. Even though it was raining.'

'The rain washed away all the houses we built,' said Mikhail.

'So we prayed and the rain stopped.'

'Then there was a drought and we had to pray to make it rain again.'

Timofei and Mikhail carried on with their procession of miracles, applying divine logic to a world in which prayer was as predictable a force as gravity; in which, in times of distress in Azerbaijan, a golden light used to spread out from the statue of Maria the Spinster, and the machines of the Communists would collapse if asked to perform an ungodly task – ploughing up the graveyards or working on the Sabbath; and in which Biblical references – Matthew 3:v 11–12, Colossians 3:v 14, Luke 14:v 27, Romans 8:v 16 – were exchanged with the precision of coordinates on a ship's bridge.

I asked them: 'Do you jump?'

'Jump?' Timofei shook his head. 'We do not jump.'

'Those Jumpers are not true Molokans,' said Mikhail.

'They claim that King David jumped.'

'Where is it written that he jumped?'

'Nowhere.'

'I've even heard them say that Christ jumped.'

There was some animated discussion about the Jumpers and their erroneous ways. Then I asked them about Kuzma.

'Kuzma? How do you know about Kuzma?'

Kuzma was a prodigious Molokan miracle-worker. I'd read something about him in Moscow.

'He was from our village,' Timofei said proudly. He then told one of the many Kuzma stories which filled the Molokan myth-store.

'Kuzma Alekseyevich was preaching the good word in the Rostov region and the Pharisees were plotting to kill him for his preaching. They tried to shoot him but the bullets went everywhere round him except where he stood – even when they were right up close. They put him in shackles and drove him down to Azerbaijan on his hands and knees. When he reached the mountains, he still wasn't dead although there was no flesh on his ankles or his wrists. So they took him by a very steep road and Kuzma prayed and the road became level. The Cossack guards were afraid so they led him to the jail and for three days sat outside his cell while inside Kuzma prayed. And he prayed so hard that the guard didn't notice when he walked free. He went up into the hills and preached to the Molokan villagers. After another three days, the Molokans went to the jail and said to the Cossacks: "Who are you guarding?" "Bad man," they said. "Who is it?" "Kuzma," said the Cossacks, and the Molokans laughed at them: "But he's preaching on the hill!"

'So the Cossacks ran up the hill but when they reached the top Kuzma had disappeared, and whenever they came to arrest him, he vanished like a rainbow. That was how it was with Kuzma.'

Mikhail took up the story: 'My grandmother said that when people travelled they would go to Kuzma to see whether their journey would be safe. He would say to them: When you reach the first bridge, you will see a Tatar riding towards you. Wave to this man because he will be a good Tatar, but at the second bridge there will be another Tatar and he will be a bad one and you must jump behind a rock.'

'Kuzma knew all the rocks.'

'He knew many things.'

'There were the earthquakes he predicted.'

'And if a fire broke out in the village, they would call him and he would come to the hut. He walked around it praying and the flames would get smaller and smaller. He would pray some more and even the smoke stopped.'

Timofei said: 'Of course he was not the only one.'

'There were always men who had the spirit.'

'I once saw a film with that Charlie Chaplin in it and he was holding up a house with one hand.'

'He must have had the same power.'

'He did, Mikhail, he did.'

In the morning, Timofei Vassiliyevich said to me: 'You must talk to my brother. He has the letter.'

'The letter?'

'The letter that tells of Kuzma's death.'

Timofei's brother lived in a Molokan community several hours away and Mikhail came too, sitting beside me on the bus which rolled like a boat as it crossed the plain. His forehead was puckered in silence, but when he told a story, or tilted at reason with one of his theories, it flattened and his face lit up. He had seen on television a programme about the mind, in which a professor spelt out the proof for the existence of a soul in man, but not in animals.

'The Molokans always knew that,' he said.

We left the bus and walked up a low hill, into the forest. After some time, Mikhail pointed down to a scattering of buildings that stretched among the trees in every direction. 'This is the village,' said Mikhail.

'It's a big village.'

'It's the biggest village in the region. In fact, it's the biggest village in Russia.'

The Molokans, a few hundred of them, lived at the far end of it. At the home of Ivan Vassiliyevich, two women were sitting in the yard. 'He's out collecting cement,' they said.

So I talked instead to his mother who was inside the house,

lying half-submerged in an old bed. She was in the last stages of an illness whose name she had no interest in knowing. She spoke for a while and then she raised a hand and we stopped talking.

A net curtain billowed at the open window. Summer sounds drifted through it – the talk of the women, the murmur of chickens, the grunt of pigs. From somewhere in the woods beyond came the 'tok-tok' of an axe. It was some time before Ivan's mother felt like speaking again.

'I was on a plane,' she said. 'We went to America. San Francisco. My cousin, she lives in America. I stayed up all night cooking for the journey because I knew what a long way it is to America. But do you know what the first thing they said to me on the aeroplane was? "Do you want breakfast?" '

'And what did you make of San Francisco?' I asked.

'Automatic! Taps, samovars, even the doors. But they keep their food locked up in bags. You can't get at it even if you're starving.'

When Ivan appeared a little later, we went outside and sat against the wall. Above our heads the net curtain blew in and out of his mother's window.

We talked for some time before I asked him about Kuzma and his miraculous feats. Then I mentioned the letter.

'What letter?'

'The letter that tells of his death.'

'My brother has it.'

'He said you have it.'

From the window came the voice of his mother: 'You have it, Ivan!'

Ivan stood and went inside and I could hear them arguing and the sound of cupboards being opened. Ivan came out again smiling and clutching in both hands a large Bible. From between its pages he extracted a number of loose sheets. A pair of blue-rimmed glasses sat at an angle on his nose, and he cleared his throat and frowned at the first sheet.

'It's very long,' he said.

'I don't mind.'

He cleared his throat. 'It begins: "Brother Arista Petrovich, Greetings to your wife, blessings on your house and your people! With great respect and love in our hearts we make the deepest bow to you –"' Ivan made a little bow. '"Akh, brother! with such impatience did we await your letter which arrived on April twenty-fourth and in which you say that it was two weeks since you became very ill. Upon hearing this we were profoundly affected by heartfelt concern, saying to ourselves – 'This is nothing other than punishment from God which often falls upon us to wake us from our deathly sinful sleep.' In these murky and troubled times we must abide always with the utmost caution and not allow the slightest wavering nor doubt in our faith and the beliefs of the Spiritual Christians passed down in the blessed memory and the visions of God of our late ancestor who lived always in the teachings and the love and forgiveness which with your own eyes you saw and with your own ears you heard during your stay with us –"'

'Perhaps we could skip the preliminaries,' I said. Ivan scanned down the page.

'No, Ivan. All of it!' His mother's voice came through the window.

Ivan made a long face and continued: '"– remember and protect us your own people and may God the Father keep you from all evil people and false teachers who with their own minds and erroneous ways corrupt the blessings of our Lord Jesus Christ and the sainted apostles –"'

He leaned forward and whispered: 'Let's leave some of this out –'

'Ivan!' cried his mother.

'Ignore her.'

But the language had captivated me. I urged him on.

'"– whose goodness was revealed to us through our ancestor Semyon Matveyevich and others during his sainted appearance among us in the time when the sun shone with holy light and the rays shone even at night-time and blessings flowed like rivers and the summer was warm and such things are thus no longer! This is a very very dangerous time and the only man who is safe is he who stands happy in the faith of the blessed word and the beliefs of the Spiritual Christians and who lives in absolute faith and love and firm hope in the word of God. Amen."

'That is the introduction,' said Ivan.

'But this *is* the right letter, Ivan? The Kuzma letter?'

'Yes – here: "Also I inform you of the great and unbearable grief, the deep and unending sorrow which is in us and in the hearts of our people and which causes us to burn and shed bitter tears each of which bears witness to his goodness. All those who came to him both in spiritual and worldly matters found him a wise doctor and his miracle-working given to him by the Grace of God shone from him as we ourselves saw and in his name the sky was covered in clouds and during his life from youth to old age, and in his wisdom and blessed courage great miracles were carried out so that there is no person who could have seen him personally and not felt respect coupled with joyfulness and awe such that even his greatest enemy could not ignore the saintliness –"'

'Kuzma's saintliness?'

Ivan raised one eyebrow behind his spectacles '"– of Starets Kuzma Alekseyevich, died by the Will of God the year eighteen sixty-three, January eighteenth, Sunday–Monday nine at night and on the nineteenth was buried in the village of Chebana."'

'Phew!' I said.

Ivan took off his blue-rimmed glasses. 'In those days, they loved to write.'

'It's a beautiful letter.'

From above came the cry: 'And the funeral, Ivan!'

'He doesn't want the funeral, Mother!'

'No, read the funeral,' I said.

He replaced his glasses. ' "The number of people at his funeral was very very many. The lunch was spread out in four huts. Extraordinary was the nature of his funeral as of all people of our time he was, by the Grace of God, a miracle-worker. They laid his blessed body in a good coffin of pine boards and carried him up to the top of the hill to a flat place near the village of Chebana. Maksim Fyodorovich was there weeping bitterly with huge tears and uncontrollable sobs. Nikolai Mikhailovich was there with his town people. We sang the eighty-seventh psalm and carried him to his grave and then the women sang the one hundred and forty-first psalm and once again our hearts filled with the deepest grief and sorrow and while we sang the psalm, and while our tears flowed, God performed a great miracle on his poor and pitiful body and it suddenly came about that the heavens descended to earth and all the air was transformed by the blessed pleasantness and joy of Heaven, and at once everything was clean and transparent, loud and resonant, so that when we finished that psalm we sang another – the eighty-third – and we sang all the way to Chebana and the sun poured down its rays onto the surface of the ground and there was a lot of mud. Inside the coffin his body was covered with the marks of countless sufferings and there was nothing but bones and stretched skin because he'd reached such a state that he could live no more yet not once did he think of himself. In discussion his words were pure. Such a man will not be seen again in all this white world and it's our grief brothers that we are left orphans without him.

'"With full hearts we carried him and not one of us was tired.

'"This letter was written by the *starets* and spiritual father Semyon Yefremovich."'

The next day was Sunday. In the chill of the early morning I walked to the prayer house. The dew was heavy on the forest path. The trees thinned and there appeared a crowd of men and women in nineteenth-century dress, converging on a freshly-painted building. Inside were already forty or fifty people seated on benches. Whenever anyone entered, they all rose and bowed. The men were gathered at one end, a sunburnt collection of low-church faces. They wore too-big suits and slab-like shoes and kept their hats under the benches. The women, facing them, wore lace and neatly pressed head-scarves.

Ivan Vassiliyevich was presiding over the *sobraniye*. He went up to the front. In turn, he called on the elders to read: Mikhail Sergeyevich! And Mikhail Sergeyevich would flick through the pages of the Bible until he found his chosen text, then read it and comment on it. Then someone would start a psalm.

The *sobraniye* lasted three hours. To begin with, it was just psalms and readings, but in time the elders paid less attention to the scriptures and became looser with their own commentary:

'Brothers, sisters, do not assume that it is easy to reach Heaven. Even here, in this room, there are many who will reach the gates only to be told the words that every Christian dreads: I do not know you . . .'

'. . . they say in schools now that we are descended from monkeys and not from God. Is it any wonder then that we behave like animals?'

'Brothers, sisters, we know that the last days are near. It is written that we should look for three signs that show it – that parents do not nourish their children, that there are many wars, and that the earth is torn apart by earthquakes. Look around you, is it not so?'

Towards the end, the benches were cleared away and a small piece of carpet was placed in the centre of the room. The elders stood on three sides of the carpet and one by one a series of individuals came up to ask for special prayers: a man whose father was in hospital, a woman whose son had a mysterious illness, and then a pair of women.

'My sister here must go to Azerbaijan,' said one of them. 'She must see our parents' grave. Pray for her please, there is no one left there, only the graves. Someone has to go to the graves of our parents. Please pray that she will be safe.'

Beside her, her sister was unable to speak through her tears.

That evening, at the house of Ivan Vassiliyevich, members of the community came and went, bringing with them bags of soft cheese and fruit and starting to talk before they had even crossed the threshold. The talking was continuous and unwavering and interrupted only when it was necessary to sing. It was close to midnight when the last of the visitors had left and Ivan pulled back his sleeve and said: 'It's time, Mikhail.'

'Yes, it's time.'

Mikhail rose from the table. He was due to visit some Molokans on the Salsk steppe. I went with him to the railway tracks. There was a place where the points changed and it was possible to board the train as it stopped. The night was close and filled with the hum of cicadas. Mikhail stood by the rails with a pilgrim's patience. I could see in the light of the moon his face set in a deep frown, but in time he looked up and smiled.

'What is it, Mikhail?'

'Doves.'

'Where?'

'Azerbaijan.'

'You had doves there?'

'I had twenty-seven. I loved my doves like the earth itself. The Baku dove is the strongest dove there is. You watch it as it spins up and up and up. You stand there looking into the sky but you cannot see it any more.'

'And now,' I asked. 'Do you still have doves?'

'No. Not now.'

Mikhail's train appeared. It was the train for Siberia. It shuddered to a halt some way up the track and we ran up along the sleepers towards it. Mikhail hauled himself up and I passed him his bag and a box of cups and plates he was taking to the newly-settled Molokans near Salsk. He stood on the footplate and we carried on talking until, away in the distance, the red light dropped to green and the carriages' couplings slammed tight.

'Goodbye!'

As the darkness took him, I heard him cry: 'Romans five, verse five!'

And hope maketh not ashamed; because the love of God
is shed abroad in our hearts . . .

In the morning I told Ivan I had to leave and he said: 'Why hurry?'

'I must reach the Turkish border before the summer ends.'

'It's a bad place there, bad people.'

'I am going to see the Doukhobors.'

'The Doukhobors?' He shook his head. 'They have a good heart. But in the head they are muddled.'

PART II

Mountain

'What do we need in order to really win? We need
three things: first – arms, second – arms, third – arms
and arms again!'

Josef Stalin addressing a workers' meeting, Tiflis, October 1905

The True Meaning of
the Stag

In Krasnodar, capital of the Kuban Cossacks, I managed to solve one of the questions that had been dogging me for weeks: where exactly is the Adygei republic?

A woman I met, herself Adygei, said: 'You're practically in it.'

She taught in a college of further education and had come up to me in a workers' café where I was wrestling with my German map. With a biro she traced a dog-leg of territory that reached down out of the mountains to kick at the outskirts of Krasnodar.

'Adygei republic. Population – four hundred and eighty-three thousand. Religion – Muslim and Christian. Seven and a half thousand square kilometres. Capital – Maikop.'

And from the Adygei republic she carried on with her biro tour, east along the Caucasus, highlighting the other non-Russian republics whose location had, until then, drawn looks of blank indifference from all those I'd asked – Karachai-Cherkessia, Kabardino-Balkaria, North Ossetia, Ingushetia.

I blamed Soviet cartophobia. While friendship between nations was encouraged, spatial awareness was not. Show a map to most post-Soviet citizens and you get a frown. But it's as much to do with the country itself – the scale of it, the numbing spaces, the changeless expanse of forest and steppe and taiga – as the transient decrees of its rulers. One nineteenth-century tsarist inspector, new to the job, started by asking a class of geography students to point out Russia on a map of the world. Not one of them could do it.

But in the offices of the Kuban Cossack choir, they were not at all shy of maps. A group of historians, working in a back-room, had been gathering information from Cossack villages. The whole of their wall was one giant map and one of the Cossacks, bullish and moustachioed, was tapping it with a stick: 'Here, steppe. Here, mountains – and along this line, between them – stanitsa ... stanitsa ... stanitsa ... stanitsa ...'.

'And these other villages,' I asked, 'to the south?'

His moustache quivered. 'Turk.'

Later that morning I left the historians. A warm wind flowed through the roadside trees. I went down to the river and fol-lowed it for some distance. Back in town, I sat bare-footed in a kiosk while one of the town's twenty thousand Armenians resoled my boots. He told me about how life is in Krasnodar; he told me how it was before. And he whispered darkly about the rise of the Cossacks.

The Kuban Cossack *voisko* has its roots in one of the oldest and most belligerent of all Cossack groups, the Zaporozhians. They came originally from the river Dnieper in the Ukraine, from the Zaporozhskaya Sich, meaning 'the clearing below the cataracts'. From here they confounded all attempts at subju-gation, made the marshland theirs and terrorised all who tried to cross it. Their raids, in dugout canoes, took them as far as Istanbul. They lived as mercenaries and pirates and dished out their loyalties to whoever it suited them at the time – Poles, Lithuanians, Russians, even Tatars. Early in the seventeenth century they helped place the False Dmitri on the Russian throne, before he was murdered and his corpse fired from a cannon.

The Zaporozhian Cossacks were the arch-Cossacks, the ones who best fulfilled that myth of the happy-go-lucky outlaw that so appealed to downtrodden Russians and Ukrainians. Gogol's Taras Bulba was a Zaporozhian. In Ilya Repin's painting *Zaporozhian Cossacks Defy the Sultan*, a group of them is gathered around a wooden table placed on the steppe. Their tonsured heads are thrown back, their extravagant moustaches draped over open mouths, all of them caught in a moment of unbridled mirth. The joke was that the Ottoman Sultan Mohammed IV, who had given himself the epithet 'Protector of Cossacks', had demanded tribute. The Cossacks, using a scribe, are dictating their response:

> Turkish Devil and Soulmate of Satan! Self-styled Lord of Christendom who is nothing of the sort! Pot-scraper of Babylon! Ale-vendor of Jerusalem! Goatherd of Alexandria! Swineherd of Upper and Lower Egypt! Sow of Armenia! Brass-necked Infidel! Go to Hell! Cossacks spit on all your present claims and any you dream up later . . .

For two centuries the Zaporozhians continued to spit at the powers around them, continued to attract the misfits of Ukrainian and Russian society, until in 1775, under Catherine the Great, the Zaporozhskaya Sich was stormed in a single night. The Cossacks scattered. Those deemed loyal to the crown were granted land of never-ploughed soil in the Kuban steppe. There they abandoned their traditional brigandry in favour of horse-breeding, fishing, and long spells of military service. They named their new capital Yekaterinodar – 'the Gift of Catherine' – and a century later, in 1894, spent 150,000 roubles on a statue of her. (The town was restyled Krasnodar – the 'Red Gift' – by the Soviets.)

In the nineteenth century, as Russia put the squeeze on the Caucasian peoples, the Kuban Cossacks were the first to help. They made up the western end of the Caucasian Line. Cossack stanitsas were established further and further into the mountains, pioneer communities designed to contain the murderous tribes, privateers defending the tsar's swollen borders. Yet even in Nicholas II's time, among the Kuban Cossacks, Ukrainian remained the language of the majority.

Their headquarters are still in Krasnodar, a few run-down buildings and a leafy courtyard. It was a sunny afternoon and I was leaning on the balustrade, following an officer as he clip-clipped across the yard on his steel-heeled boots, as he jogged up the steps with a jangle of webbing. He was the *esaul* of the Kuban host, the ataman's deputy, and he was called Shotkin.

'You'll have to be quick.' He drew back his sleeve. 'I have a meeting in exactly five minutes.'

We stepped into his office. He threw his cap on a hook, tugged at the knees of his breeches and sat down. His desk was empty. He opened a drawer, which was also empty. He found a blank sheet of paper which he placed in front of him. 'Five minutes!'

'I wanted to ask you about how you see the role of today's Cossack.'

He was staring at me, blinking.

'Whether perhaps with the growth of nationalist feelings in this region you see an opportunity to reinstate the Cossacks as a kind of buffer between Russia and the peoples of the Caucasus.'

'Eh?'

'Like the old Caucasian Line –'

'The Caucasian Line?'

'Yes.'

'What line?'

'During the Caucasian wars there –'

He raised his hand. 'Enough!'

'We have three minutes left.'

He crushed the paper into a ball and lobbed it into the bin. 'Huh!' The legs of his chair scraped on the wooden floor. 'To my house!'

Shotkin was already ushering me out. He locked the door and straightened his cap. His meeting he dismissed with an arbitrary grunt and together we marched out towards the gate.

I liked Shotkin. His self-importance seemed just as much a joke to him as it did to me. He had a lovely moustache, which tumbled down his upper lip and bulged into bells of grey on either side of his chin. His eyes under his cap were bright and unquestioning. As we strode briskly along the avenue towards his house, he told me that his great-grandfather had looked after the young Nicholas II until he was four; and I remembered the pictures of Nicholas's son, the Tsarevich Aleksei, frail and sickly in the arms of a giant Cossack.

Shotkin lived in part of an old pre-Revolutionary town villa, painted sky blue and guarded by a dog so fierce that I had to wait across the street while he tied it up.

'Its mother killed a man!' boasted Shotkin. 'So would this one, if I gave it half a chance.'

Before long, in his high-ceilinged sitting-room, Shotkin had arranged before me two swords, a pigskin knout, a *beshmet* tunic, a *cherkesska* (heavy with medals), two *papakha* (high astrakhan hats), a *bashlyk* (red dress hood) and a *burkha* (a stiffened woollen sleeveless cape which you climb inside like a neck-high sentry-box). He pulled out a drawer full of identity cards, and like a master of ceremonies reeled off the posts he had held – major in a rocket regiment! Member of the Cossack Congress! Commander of the Kuban *voisko*! Cossack adviser to the Duma! Officer of the Kuban Housing Committee!

'I've got millions of titles!'

His photographs were an equal source of pleasure – Shotkin with Patriarch Aleksei II in Nizhny Novgorod, Shotkin with the Russian basketball team, Shotkin flanked by bikinied beauty queens, Shotkin at a funeral for Cossacks killed in Moldova, Shotkin at a regimental parade.

'Look how my medals are pulling me down. Hoo-yurr! Sometimes when I wear them I am staggering with their weight.'

He leapt around the room, pulling his *shashka* from its scabbard, slamming a bottle and glasses on the table: 'Hundred grams!' and thrusting one hand down inside his belt, rocking back on his heels and raising his glass: 'Lords, elders! A word in Church Slavonic – a song for the troops: Rally round, *kazaky* . . .'

And all the while, on a high shelf above his head, was the photograph of another man, a grey-suited man at a desk, an *apparatchik* who stared at the camera with the comfortable stare of a *petit chef*. This was the man, the Party member, who could not be seen in church, who was forced to stand beneath the trees while his wife lit a candle in the cathedral for his dead father, who wore his suit lightly with the ideas of the state, and when the time came in 1990 found no difficulty at all in shaking them off for his *cherkesska*, his grey bulging moustache and the rediscovered zeal of the Cossack revival.

There was no contradiction for Shotkin. 'At the beginning we didn't know whether they'd put us in prison or shoot us.'

He was searching in a cupboard for something. Finding it, he crossed the room and sat down. He held a letter from the Ministry of the Interior; attached to it was a copy of a death certificate dated 13 January 1938. Cause of Death: Shot.

'My grandfather.' Shotkin was suddenly subdued. 'He was the last ataman of his stanitsa. He built them a school and they shot him. My father too, they called him an enemy of the people and worried him until he died.'

Shotkin looked at me. An incredulous sadness played in the innocence of his face. For a moment we were silent in that high-ceilinged room. Through the open window came a breeze which scuffed at the hem of the curtain. The sun was bright on the wall across the street and from somewhere in the distance, in another house, we heard the sound of a door slamming, a dog barking, shouts of greeting.

Shotkin stood and went to the kitchen. I heard him mumbling to himself. When he came back, he was clutching bread and tomatoes and a lump of pig fat. He had recovered his high spirits. 'You're not a Mussulman, are you?'

'No.'

'Of course not. Your queen, she's a Christian. And I've seen your bacon – meat, fat, meat, fat . . . you starve the pig, you feed the pig, you starve it, you feed it. With us' – he slapped the unbroken white of the fat – 'we just feed it!'

Shotkin put me onto an engineer who was driving up out of Krasnodar to Maikop, into the Adygei republic. With him were his wife and an elderly Cossack they called Uncle Sasha. Uncle Sasha had a briar of a beard which was pressed against his tunic. He'd been to a *krug* and he was snoring loudly. In the early afternoon we left the road and bumped up a track to a small clearing.

Green midsummer hung in that roadside glade; flies buzzed in the grass. The engineer's wife swilled out the cups and Uncle Sasha stretched, yawned and pulled from his pocket a piece of smoked sturgeon. He added this to the food on the car's bonnet.

Had we, I asked, crossed the Adygei border yet?

'Border?' said the engineer.

'What border?' Uncle Sasha stood to attention. 'It might be here.' Then he leapt to another spot, 'Or it might be here!'

The jokes continued for a time while the notion of independence for these little north Caucasian republics was dismissed.

'And Chechnya?' I asked.

The laughing subsided. Chechnya's different. Why, they could not say. And what about these other peoples, too – the Karachai, the Balkars, the Kabards, the Ossetes, the Ingush. They shrugged at these names. The whole subject was too serious to be taken seriously in public. They unpacked more food, and with the food the harmless chatter resumed; in Russia there is no anxiety so great that it cannot find relief in a full table.

After eating and drinking we sat on the grass and Uncle Sasha stood by the car and, with his leather top-boots shuffling in the dust, sang a song: 'O, the man I'd like to marry, he should wear a plain white dicky, white and plain . . .'

Then from a kit bag he retrieved a stack of books. He gave me a copy. 'It is my own book. I wrote it.' On the cover, with the cross-hairs of a rifle's sights at its centre, was the figure of a woman. On her head was a forage cap, and she wore epaulettes on her shoulders. Apart from that she was naked.

'It is a memoir of fighting in Poland.'

'Nonsense, Uncle Sasha!' said the engineer. 'It's just a fantasy.'

'It's how things were then. You're too young to know.'

The book was called *Wild Sex in the Bunker of War*.

In Maikop the sun was very bright. Children were licking ice cream in its glare. Beneath the trees, men sat in twos and threes fingering their prayer beads. Being an old Cossack stronghold, the town was laid out in a precise grid. Uncle Sasha made a chopping motion with his hand: 'They made these streets with the slashes of a sabre.'

But to me Maikop was at once remarkable for three things: the 126 banks which had sprung up in the last few years, the brand-new mansions that ringed the town, and the hills. The hills were in themselves not that remarkable – nothing compared to the mountains out of sight beyond them – but after months in the steppe they appeared to me like the first few days of spring.

I stayed that night with Uncle Sasha and the engineer and his wife. It was hot and we sat outside. Uncle Sasha's mother joined us with the engineer's daughter and his two-month-old grandchild. To these five generations were added through the evening neighbours and cousins who drifted in to sit beneath the vines. The talk was the anxious talk of a frontier people whose dominance was suddenly in question.

It was the Americans, said one, the Americans have destabilised our country. Gorbachev was a spy. The whole thing's a conspiracy of the committee of international Jewish bankers. I could not help laughing.

'But surely,' he said, 'you have read *The Protocols of the Elders of Zion*?'

The next day was Saturday. On the edge of the town I found a small church where a baptism was in progress. It was a complicated business as several generations were being baptised at once. The poor priest would call for the mother of the applicant, only to be told that she too wanted to be baptised. He found it all rather muddling.

They stood in a wide semi-circle in front of him. Their foreheads were wet and they held candles.

'Now, crossing,' explained the priest. 'It is very important to do it like this. The Catholics and the Armenian Gregorians do it like this, which is wrong. You must do it like this. You do this in front of each of the icons, and when you pray.' Stepping up to each one of them with a pair of scissors, he asked: 'Are you Russian?'

'Yes, I'm Russian', they replied, and he cut off a piece of hair. 'Russian, yes.'

'Of course.'

'I'm Polish.'

'That's all right. We're all Slavs.'

'I'm Finnish.'

'Hmm.' But he blessed her anyway and snipped her hair, and, the semi-circle complete, took his place again in front of them.

'Now, let's see that this isn't the last time you come to church. Come on Sundays and not just on holidays. Remember, this is the Russian Church, your native Church –'

One of the newly-baptised boys took out a cigarette. 'Psst!' He winked to his neighbour.

'– it is your inheritance. The Church is like your own land and you must protect it. We Russians are not like these Americans and Germans and English who come with fifty million dollars and build their churches and then hand out leaflets. Do you think they'd do that if not for their own gain? Do you think so? No! They will come back later and take all our oil and gas. So you must always –'

'Come on,' whispered the boy. 'Let's go.'

Uncle Sasha told me about a certain Victor Grigoryevich. 'A great expert on Cossacks.'

Victor Grigoryevich was wearing overalls, standing hands-on-hips at one of Maikop's cement-splashed building sites. He was directing a delivery of gutter-pipes at his brother's fifteen-roomed, three-storeyed mansion. When I asked him what his brother did, the answer was a laconic 'Business.'

Victor felt strongly about the Cossacks. We sat on piles of bricks in the late sun and he squinted at me from behind tinted spectacles. The British he did not like. His uncle had fought for the Axis under Shkuro, had worn the wolfskin cap, and died when they were all returned to Stalin in 1945. It was the British who sent them back. 'You know that?'

'Yes.'

'Do you?'

I assured him I did, but he continued to eye me suspiciously. We got on better in the speculative realms of ancient history. An advocate of the tenuous Cossack–Scythian link, Victor began to speak of the Maikop *kurgan*. In 1898, 360 sacrificed horses had been unearthed around a tomb (confirming thereby some of Herodotus's anecdotal descriptions of Scythian burials). He spoke with verve about the Maikop vases and the animal style – that exuberant zoomorphic art that saw Scythian shields and buckles carved with fantastic beasts, the same beasts which in tattoos adorned the skin of their chieftains, and which in time migrated up through Scandinavia to appear in the margins of Celtic manuscripts. And he talked about the stag. It was the stag, he said, that interested him most of all; and in this at least we found a mutual enthusiasm.

I too had been drawn to the stag of all the Scythian motifs – to the exuberance of the grinning Pazyryk stag with his elongated antlers, to the plaque stags, the belt stags, the stags appliquéd on pale felt, but most of all to the shield stag which had been found in the stanitsa of Kostromskaya in the Kuban steppe. In this version, sixth century BC or earlier, pure gold, the stag's head is raised. An extravagant squiggle of antlers runs down his back. His straining neck, his flared nostrils, his wide, startled eye all bring to mind that moment when he detects the hunter for the first time. But beneath the stag, the legs are bunched up. Some have suggested that the beast is in full chase; more convincing to me is the theory that the legs are bound, in preparation for sacrifice.

In his *Natural History*, Pliny records the belief that stags are able to lure snakes with their breath, then hoof them to death. Stags were also able to ward off the evil eye, and for both these traits they became an accepted representation of Christ. Hubert is the patron saint of hunters, having had revealed to him in the forest a white hart with a crucifix suspended between its antlers. In pre-history, antlers were used widely in totemic rites, and their remains have been found at sacred sites from York-shire to Tibet. Not long ago Siberian shamans were still known to take on a stag identity. In Siberian mythology it is the stag that carries away the souls of the dead. The Scythian tombs at Pazyryk contained sets of gold-antlered head-dresses so that sacrificed horses could, in that other world, become stags. The ancient Saka peoples of Central Asia – whose name itself may derive from '*sag*', the word for stag in some Iranian tongues – were said to have taken the stag as their totem. Groups of young Saka used to rove the steppe beneath the banner of the stag.

Victor's own theories about the Cossacks' link with the stag cult concurred at this point. 'The name "cossack",' he claimed, 'came from an old Iranian term meaning white stag – "*sack*" being the word for stag.'

And white stags were the standard gift to the Chinese court by a number of Central Asian peoples.

Whatever the validity of such theorising – and what better way to while away an evening in the north Caucasus? – the stag remains the perfect symbol for the Cossacks: fleet of foot, combative, flamboyantly male. It is no surprise that the emblem of the largest of all Cossack groups, the Don *voisko* – sewn into their banners, set into commemorative stones – is a stag, its side pierced by an arrow.

Victor's brother pulled up at the site in a black BMW. I watched them discuss progress. Above them, the low sun glowed red on the brickwork. It glowed silver on the ornate, galvanised bargeboard (the characteristic of these sudden southern palaces), and it glowed on the fretwork which rose at each corner of the house to a finial of a leaping stag.

* * *

To counter Victor's Cossack claims on the ancient world, I sought out an Adygei archaeologist.

I found Adam Kerashev in more traditional surroundings – on the fifth floor of a Brezhnevite apartment block. The block stood among a phalanx of others. At their bases were children scrabbling in the dust, men tending rows of tomato plants and women beating carpets.

Adam Kerashev was a great enthusiast. He wore a woollen hat throughout the morning and sat on a sofa with his leg stretched out along the cushions. He had injured it in the mountains but retained, in his upper body, the lively movements of a spaniel.

'You ask about deer. All over the mountains you will see these standing stones, in Russian "*alyeni kamni*" – the deer stones. They were totems for warriors.'

But about the Cossacks' claim to be indigenous he was dismissive. 'The Cossacks are migrants. The Adygei people have lived in this area since the earliest times.' He pointed to a glass-fronted cabinet. 'Look at that.'

I slid back the glass doors and pulled out a photographic print of a circular design.

'This motif was on a plate I dug up last summer. It is inlaid with the teeth of wild boar. This is our pantheon. Here, you see the rays spreading out over the plate – this is the sun, always the central part of Adygei faith. Next, the earth. Then the trinity. And fourth is this, which is a representation of Alexander.'

'Alexander the Great?'

He nodded.

'And Islam?'

'The Adygei became Muslim for political reasons. But at our heart we are mountain people, and mountain people always worship what they see around them.'

Wincing, he adjusted his leg on the sofa. 'We worship not

only the sun and the peaks but the copper-age barrows. Even until quite recently, the Adygei used to conduct ceremonies at these graves.' Adam gave an animated version of the ceremonies. 'The people would stand outside around the pile of stones and, in secret, the chiefs would send a little boy into the shaft. He would crawl in, like this' – Adam slumped down onto the floor – 'and cry out. All the people would look at the stones and think it was the soul of the dead one. The boy howling: whaa-ah!'

His wife came running in from the kitchen. 'What . . . Adam, get up from the floor!'

Adam slunk back to his convalescence. He sat there contrite and thwarted. Last summer he had found dozens of new mounds to dig, and had spent several months preparing to excavate them.

'But now tell me, how am I to go digging this season with such a leg?'

Walking back into town I came across a building with a plaque fixed to the wall: 'In this house, on 18–21 September 1891 the great writer A.M. Gorky was held under arrest.' Beside the inscription was the great writer himself – in profile, hair swept back, chin raised, staring down the road with the determined look of a good revolutionary.

An elderly Russian woman came and tapped me on the arm as I copied the inscription.

'Do you understand what's written?'

'Yes.'

'Not that.' She swept Gorky away with a flick of her hand. 'That sort of writing is only sinful. The Bible, in the Bible.' She searched my face for signs of agreement. 'Is your Bible a Mussulman Bible?'

'No.'

'Then you will know. You will know that there's no avoiding what's going to happen.'

From the pocket of her housecoat projected a bottle of vodka.

The Forests of Romantika

At dawn the next day I left Maikop and its half-built palaces, and the songs of Uncle Sasha and the warring archaeologists, and with a map pencil-ringed with stanitsas, took a bus into the hills. The morning sun rose from wooded slopes into a sky of the deepest blue. The Belaya river rushed beside the road, clogging the bridges with its detritus of broken trees. And above it all, like a rising moon, appeared the first snowcap of the Great Caucasus.

At once an argument began. A woman wanted the window closed; the man in front of her did not.

'I thought you were a decent woman.'

'What?'

'Going on about the window like that.'

'I'm ill. I can't have the cold blowing in on me.'

'You're ill because you're so twisted and angry.'

She said nothing.

'Kind people don't get ill like that.'

'Everyone gets ill.'

'Not like that, they don't.'

When later she got off the bus, a murmuring consensus spread through it: 'Refugee – Armenian – Georgian . . .'

A side road left the valley and doubled back to climb up the slopes. I walked for a while and then a hay truck took me over the ridge. The truck turned into the fields and the driver extended a finger towards the yellow ribbon of a road. Some way up it, I'd been told, was the stanitsa of Novosvobodnaya and an ataman by the name of Volodya. The road led there and nowhere else. Its houses were obscured by fruit trees. In the square two men were hosing down a carpet.

I greeted them. 'Good morning!'

There was no response.

A red-faced man was staring at me from the middle of the square. He held a pig on a piece of string. To one side, beneath some lime trees, was a group of women sitting beside the well.

'Where might I find Ataman Volodya?'

The ones with the carpet paused with their hosing. 'Dunno.'

The one with the pig left the square. One of the women said: 'You'd be advised to go. We don't like strangers here.'

I looked around the square, thanked the women, and left that stanitsa by the same road.

That evening I reached a place called Romantika. At one time it had been a monastery, but during the Soviet period it had shaken off the dust of centuries to welcome the masses. It had become a mountain resort.

At the gatehouse a dwarf in a sheepskin was dozing on a motorcycle; inside the compound, the distant sound of goat-bells broke the stillness of the evening. Otherwise the place was deserted.

Nothing fades quite so quickly nor so tackily as a Soviet resort. Through a narrow unglazed window, I looked in at what had once been a theatre, at the wattle boards that curled from the ceiling, the broken glass that covered the seats. Someone had charcoaled an Orthodox cross on the wall. Across the stage was a loose scattering of bottles.

Beyond the old monastery buildings was the hostel. A car was parked in front of it. Two men were trying to light a fire.

There was a small stack of wood beside them and bloody slabs of raw meat on newspaper. Lying back on a rug was a woman reading a book. She turned on her side to watch me as I approached. The men gave me some food, and I slept in the old hostel in a room without windows. I could hear the men and the woman on the rug long into the night.

In the morning, I walked back out of the monastery gates. Dew lay thickly in the woods. The vaults of the forest met above the road and only in patches was the sun able to shine through. Then the trees thinned and the ground fell away and in the distance was wave upon wave of blue ridges dropping to the steppe.

For a week or more I wandered east along the edge of the Caucasus, out of the Adygei republic, back into Russia, up into the mountains, back out onto the steppe. In the uplands, the people were thick-limbed and fluent in their movements. They tended towards silence. The ends of their sentences would drift away, leaving them to squint like sailors into the expanse all around them. The higher up they lived the more silent they became until, I imagined, beyond the stanitsas and the Circassian aouls, they would become indistinguishable from the Caucasian cliffs themselves.

The valleys were flat, covered with wheat fields and rye fields and sunflowers. Groves of willow bordered the rivers; the first slopes of the hills rose to ridges of thick forest. A plump fertility hung over everything. On the edge of one stanitsa I met a woman grazing her cow in knee-high grass. 'Squeeze these hills,' she said, 'and you can drink the juice that comes out. Even a fool could live off this land.'

Which, of course, is not quite true. It proved just as easy to starve people here as it did in the Ukraine. Robert Conquest, in his *Harvest of Sorrow*, quotes the account of a soldier entering a stanitsa down here in the early 1930s. Twenty thousand people lived in the stanitsa, but that day it was silent. The soldier wandered among the cabins, the untilled plots. In some of the houses there were people in bed. In one a couple was sitting together hand in hand. But in the whole of that stanitsa, on a bright spring day, he found only one person alive – a man squabbling with some cats over the carcass of a pigeon.

Just before the Great Famine a strange thing happened. Ordered to surrender their livestock to the collective farms, these southern villagers tried to sell them. The prices collapsed, so they slaughtered the animals and ate them. For the first time in history, it was said, Russian peasants had their fill. Enter a kitchen at this time and whole families would swivel their heads towards you, their mouths running with fat, their cheeks swollen with half-chewed meat.

Then there was no livestock and no meat. Nothing to till the fields. From the towns came larger and larger demands for grain, and more and more brutal methods of getting it. The peasants starved in regions which are among the most fertile on earth. They sucked on birch leaves and grass. They boiled their boots, but they still starved. They starved at barricades put up to keep them out of built-up areas. (Few in the towns knew what was happening.) They starved while all around them were fields thick with grain, from which they were prohibited on pain of death, and which in large part were guarded by young Pioneers – children – who would chant:

> We take the thieves to jail
> To intimidate the foe!
> We guard the village soil
> To let the harvest grow!

Voices of dissent were few, and quickly silenced. But one who survived writing a letter of protest to Stalin was Mikhail

Sholokhov, Don Cossack, Party-approved writer, Nobel Prize-winner and author of *And Quiet Flows the Don.* Stalin's response was unequivocal: 'the esteemed grain-growers have waged what was virtually a "quiet" war against Soviet power. A war of starvation, dear Comrade Sholokhov . . .'

So, the inverted logic of the dictator, the psychopath's paranoia: it's not me doing it to them, but them to me; I'm not starving them, they're trying to starve me.

Churchill, on hearing that collectivisation had entailed the deaths of ten million 'small men', commented: 'A generation will no doubt come to whom their miseries were unknown, but it will be sure of having more to eat and bless Stalin's name.'

The way to the stanitsa of Abadzheskaya led down an avenue of Lombardy poplars so straight it was like walking down the colonnade of some great temple. On the edge of the village I fell into step with a man pushing a pram: 'We will always survive. We are like bears in the forest.' In the pram was a neatly stacked pile of birch logs. I asked him who I should speak to in the stanitsa and he directed me to the house of Nikolai Grigoryevich Gulenko.

Nikolai Grigoryevich was sitting on a log in his yard, watching his chained-up dog chew on a bone. He was an elderly Cossack with gentle manners and a sad face and when he saw me, announcing myself from beyond his wicket gate, he uncoiled himself from the log and greeted me like an old friend.

We went inside to his sitting room, through a mud-floored kitchen where his wife was rolling pastry. His wife was called Darya Daniilovna, but they addressed each other as 'Grandmother' and 'Grandfather'.

Nikolai spoke softly. He sat slightly forward in an old armchair. He'd joined the Cossack movement when it began, in the far-off heady days of 1990.

'All my life I'd wanted to be a Cossack – not because I wanted to fight. Just because I knew that's what I was, a Cossack. But at the second meeting, I looked around and saw the faces of men that were cruel. They were the faces of my childhood.'

Nikolai was born in 1917 into a dangerous world. War had drained the south of its former wealth and, come the Revolution, the region collapsed into a series of fractured loyalties – Bolsheviks and the Volunteer Army, *frontoviki* and Circassians, Red Cossacks and White Cossacks. Briefly, in 1918, the Whites gained control. But with their defeat in 1920 came retribution. The death squads of the Cheka worked through the stanitsas. Many Cossacks reverted to the old ways. They became outlaws, shaggy-haired wanderers, steppe bandits who rode in at night and raided farms and held up grain convoys. Those who fled the country, leaving behind them the shattered certainties of the tsarist empire, now loitered in the backstreets of Istanbul, worked as doormen in Paris night-clubs, or performed spectacular stunts of horsemanship in travelling shows while the office-workers of French and English towns whistled and applauded.

Nikolai remembered the end of the 1920s in the south. 'The first to go was anyone with more animals, anyone who could read. This was 1928 –'

'1929, *Dyedushka!*' came a voice from the kitchen.

'Was it? I was still a boy. I watched from my window at night, all those men being put in lorries. Took away just as many as they could fit on their lorries.'

'Where to?'

'As far as they could. Beyond the Urals. They took them there and left them without anything. It was the middle of winter, hundreds of miles on every side of them. It was like killing them outright. We saw none of those ones again.'

Nikolai himself was taken in 1931. With his father, mother, brother and sister, he was driven out into the steppe and left in a house without doors or windows. Being enemies of the people, they were not allowed to work. They had with them a sack of grain and when it was empty they took to going out at night scouring the edge of the roads for loose seeds. In that way they collected enough to make a few griddle-cakes. They managed to save a little for the winter. But then the activists came and took even that.

'Sometimes you heard a scratching at the door at night, and that was the orphans looking for food. In the morning you would find them in the yard or in the road, lying where they fell. What could we do? We had nothing. We were practically dead too.'

Nikolai and his family survived like this for two years.

Darya Daniilovna appeared in the doorway, wiping her hands on her apron. 'They used to come to our houses with pointed sticks. They stabbed at the walls and the mattresses and in the stables looking for food. Everyone was hungry, and they just took away all the food.'

'And you,' I asked her, 'were you sent into exile?'

'My family were taken. But as for me, my grandmother hid me. A year and a half I was hidden in her house, in the attic. The soldiers never came there. I watched them through the cracks in the boards, with their pointed sticks poking at the walls.'

In 1935 Nikolai Grigoryevich returned to the stanitsa. 'My father had to live in the woods to avoid people's eyes.'

But a year later, everything began to ease up. At the end of 1936, the new Soviet Constitution – on paper a model of fairness – guaranteed the rights of Cossacks. Some were still frightened, but others began to get out their old things and on holidays would go and visit each other's houses in a *papakha* or a *cherkesska*.

'In the evening you'd hear the old Cossack songs being sung.

The officers were there with the accordions. They told their stories and I was still young and thought: what a world they'd known, and felt certain it would come again.'

Nikolai frowned and looked down at the palm of his hand. 'But all the time the cadres were watching them. A year later all these Cossacks were arrested. They were always very clever like that, the cadres.'

26 September 1937 was a Sunday. Nikolai was chopping wood when the activists came. 'Where is your father?' they asked.

'I was only twenty and I dared to ask, "And where is your warrant?" But they had one.' Nikolai looked away. 'Of course they had one. They went into the woods and found him.'

It was the day hundreds were arrested; they shot Nikolai's father a month later.

Darya Daniilovna came in from the kitchen with a plate of *pelmeni*. 'All because he wouldn't be an informer.' She shook her head. 'Eat, eat. Come on, you're hungry.'

We ate in silence. Two of the walls were hung with carpets, and on one was a pair of ceremonial *shashky*. Nikolai was sitting beneath them. Darya was on a stool beside him. He was subdued and his food lay untouched before him.

He leaned forward and began to talk again. There was one thing, one thing above all, that had stayed with him, and now he would tell me. It was not the guilt he felt for his father's death, nor the years foraging on the steppe, nor any of those years of Stalin's purges. It was one night in 1921 when he was only four years old.

At that time, just after the Civil War, each community had its own group of fighters. One evening they agreed to gather for a *krug*. 'Dress up,' their ataman said. 'Wear your finest clothes – it's a special occasion!'

The Cossacks gathered at the council. They found there a large group of Cheka guards. At once they were ordered to take off their clothes. They were led out naked onto the green. One hundred and eighteen men.

'I was awake. That night we all heard a terrible noise. It wasn't a human noise. It was a noise like animals . . .' Nikolai put his face in his hands; he was weeping. 'I am sorry . . . I am sorry.'

The Cossacks, he said, were not shot. On the green the Cheka had brought out a machine that was used for killing pigs. Each of the Cossacks was put into it and beheaded.

Later we went out into Nikolai's small yard. He had put on his *cherkesska* and a ceremonial *papakha*. 'It was my father's.'

He stood by the gate. The uniform looked out of place on him. He mumbled things I could not hear. As I left, he gripped my arm and looked at me with heavy eyes. 'May God guide you through your work. Don't ever let the truth leave your sight.'

A Cossack Wedding

It was a warm evening. The town of Labinsk hummed with the expectancy of a pre-concert audience. There was the sound of traffic and a dairy, and somewhere far off the brass and thump of a military band. I was in the main square waiting to meet a 'folklorist', and while waiting I had fallen in with a couple of Cossacks sitting on a bench, father and son, who had come in from their stanitsa for a horse sale.

'There's been a bit of a celebration here today,' the father said.

'What was the occasion?' I asked.

'That I couldn't tell you.'

'An old battle, more than likely, father.'

The old man pursed his lips and nodded.

During the early Soviet years, Labinsk had been such a hotbed of dissent that the authorities were obliged to deport its entire population. Now in the main square, above our heads, a Russian flag and a Cossack flag flew side by side on the roof of the Mir cinema. Slogans cried from the walls:

PEACE, BEAUTY, LOVE AND TRUTH – THE
    GUIDING STARS OF COSSACKDOM!
RE-ESTABLISH THE HONOUR OF THE
    COSSACKS!
I LOVE YOU, RUSSIA, MY DEAR RUS!

In the still evening air, the old man sighed and started talking of his own stanitsa and its haytime heartiness, and its swift horses and apple-cheeked girls, and its connection with the great rebel Kochubey which, being mumbled, I took to be a tenuous one.

'I imagine you know about our Kochubey?' he said.

I told him I had been in Kochubeyevskoe and had seen the rebel's square-jawed bust and his pugnacious face. I had read too the story of this Red Cossack who had had his status as folk hero sealed not only in a bronze bust in an eponymous stanitsa, but in the pages of a novel. Few households in the Kuban were without Arkady Peventsev's *Kochubey*. That its hero was a Red, a martyr for the Bolsheviks who subsequently did their best to wipe out the Cossacks, mattered less than that he was a fiery Kuban Cossack who couldn't read or write but was able to leap into the saddle from a standing position.

After the 1917 Revolution, Kochubey had become the rallying-point for those Cossacks opposed to General Denikin's Whites. His roving army operated behind enemy lines, driving the 'bloodsuckers' time and again from their positions. But in the end the Whites reduced them to a force of just fourteen men who were caught trying to flee through the blizzard-swept Kalmyk desert. Kochubey's men were hacked to death with sabres. He himself was spared. They gave him quarters and staff and a spongy-mattressed bed. Denikin came and offered him the rank of colonel if he joined the Whites. Kochubey refused. He told the general he would be pleased to cut his throat. They took him and hanged him with a plywood board pinned to his chest: 'Red Bandit Kochubey!'

The younger Cossack looked out across the square. 'But there was White Kochubeys too, father.'

'There was Kochubeys of all kinds.'

'You said Pushkin wrote about one.'

'He did. The one tied up with Mazepa, according to history. And there was another Kochubey who went to Africa.'

'Africa?'

'He started a crocodile farm there. But it didn't work.'

'I suppose it's a difficult business, father, crocodile farming.'

'It's not easy.'

The folklorist, when he arrived, turned out to be affiliated to the Ethnographic Institute in Moscow. He went by the name of Misha Yefremovich. He was a pale-faced, intense man in his forties, given to sudden bursts of enthusiasm. He called himself a Kuban Cossack, in that his grandmother was a Kuban Cossack and he had spent his summers down here as a child. To him Cossackdom was a storehouse of unsullied tradition to which his blood and his learning had combined to give him the key.

Standing at his desk in a bare-walled office he wasted no time in expounding his main thesis: that the Cossacks were the heirs to the greatest technological breakthrough in history.

'What would you say is traditionally closest to the heart of a Cossack? His *voisko*? His stanitsa? What do you think?'

'His sword?'

Misha leaned towards me theatrically. 'His horse!'

He began to spell out the effect that riding had had on history: the way mounted archers replaced the more cumbersome chariots, and that rumours of their existence led the Greeks to invent a new beast – the centaur – to explain them. As with war, so with agriculture: whereas a man on foot can tend to seventy sheep at most, a man on horseback can look after seven hundred.

While it is hard to dispute that riding a horse – rather than merely harnessing it – was developed by people living in this region, and that, yes, perhaps no other single act had such a far-reaching effect on history, I told him that I did not believe the Cossacks could prove a blood link with these early horsemen, or anyone else for that matter.

149

'I'm not talking of proof!' Misha said. 'Look around you! Can you think of anyone who knows the horse better than us Cossacks?'

I asked Misha about getting to the mountain stanitsas and he said I was in luck. He was going to a wedding in Besleneyevskaya the following day.

On a morning of high blue skies we left Labinsk and headed through a long poplar avenue towards the hills. At one point there appeared at the roadside a vast Soviet construction of rough-cast flying swans, vine leaves and a plaited woman proffering bread and salt; beside them was a steel plate painted with the words: 'Stanitsa est. 1861'.

In that settlement we called in on Ilya, Misha's cousin. He was sleeping on a bench outside his house. A cat lay on the mound of his stomach. When he awoke he scooped away the cat, swung his legs down and, scratching his beard, pointed to a pile of new bricks. 'Almost lost them all.'

The bricks had been delivered for the new church. In the night Ilya had heard his dog barking and a shout, and this morning he had found scattered by the gate a quantity of bricks and a bloodied square of denim. He held up the piece of cloth: 'I wouldn't call these people Cossacks, would you? When I was young we would steal gates as a joke. But bricks for a church?'

Ilya was also due at the wedding, and we gave him a lift.

The plain became a steep-sided valley. In places cliffs broke through the forest but for the most part the slopes were cushioned with green. At their foot, the trees gave way to fields of half-mown grass which stretched across the valley floor. Misha was talking about Cossack marriage traditions as if they were some sort of manifesto.

'Cossacks have always loved the free life, the *volnitsa*. If they wanted to they would sleep together before marriage. It was perfectly natural to share a bed, although it was rare for a girl to surrender her virtue until they were married.'

That said, in Cossack dialects words for weapons and species of fish are matched in number only by those for an illegitimate child. When the men were seen returning from war, the whole stanitsa would drop their tools and go to greet them. The young wives would kneel before the horses of their husbands and thank them for his safe return, and if she did not lift her eyes to his, it was understood she had not been faithful, and if she did not come to greet him at all, it meant that neither was she sorry about it. And the sayings were used to urge restraint in his beating: 'The green grape is not sweet, sir ... young reason is not strong...'

The stanitsa of Besleneyevskaya lay beside the Hodz river, a muddy collection of dwellings around the old kolkhoz buildings. Ilya led us to a row of huts neatly divided from each other by wattle fencing. A table stood outside one of the huts and scattered around it – standing, sitting, lying in the grass – was a group of villagers. Someone was playing an accordion and there was gravelly laughter from one end of the table; the couple themselves sat at the other end half-screened by bottles and flowers, and in silence.

'Ilya!' A man with a yellow moustache grabbed Misha's cousin and kissed him on the lips. Ilya shoved him aside and reached for one of the bottles; Misha started explaining some of the 'folklore aspects' of the gathering.

In this way the afternoon passed, a protracted bout of eating and drinking, accordion-playing and reminiscing. The cloud came down from the mountains, then thinned and broke and the sun rolled free and picked out the pearly frock of the bride. She stifled a yawn. At four o'clock she looked across at her husband and they stood to leave. They were going back to Stavropol. They lived and worked there, and had done for some years. As the bride peeled away the tentacles of her grand-mother's embrace, the groom put on a pair of dark glasses and went to start the car. He turned it on the grass and opened the door for his bride and they headed off down the valley where, in a scuff of dust, they disappeared behind the hills.

The party continued. Evening pushed into the garden and I found myself surrounded by a fever of long-held fury.

'The Cossacks were a mess on the floor, and they just wiped us up!'

'Destroyed us like we was a class.'

'Took our bread and let us starve.'

Maksim, sitting opposite me, was a sun-creased, chuckling old man who started a long monologue about his time in the thirties.

'The Party sent round their comrades but unfortunately not all them comrades were very comradely. They was agitators – and this was the kind of agitating they did: if you don't want to work on the collective farm voluntary, fine, you can work under the knout. It ended when they came to take my father. Twelfth of February, it was –'

'What was the year, Maksim?' I asked.

'Year?' he drew on his cigarette. 'How should I know what year? It was the twelfth of February, that's all. Anyway, they had an order to arrest my father and they did. Then after two weeks they came for us little ones. This high we were, and they put us in wagons with lots of other children. In Pyatigorsk we were on a train and they painted great big letters on the train: "VOLUNTARY MIGRANTS". And just in case these volun-tary migrants ran away, they gave us guards with rifles.

'I met up with my father and a lot of other voluntary migrants and we all went off to the Perm Oblast in the north Urals. That was how they tried to destroy the Cossacks and that was how they built their new Russia – sent people to chemical works and dynamo works and built canals, and all of it on a crust of bread and a pair of wooden boots.'

I asked him what he remembered of Perm.

'Oh, we had a life up there, couple of cows, wooden house, and us kids used to go off and play in a church. There was a big bell, size of a kitchen. Five or six of us would get on the bell and swing it. You could see out across this flat plain – they said it was mountains up there but they don't know what mountains are – and when we swung it the noise was like a bong!–bong!–bong! and so loud there was some boys couldn't stand on their feet. One day we went up to the church and the men were cutting up the bell. Said it was for a tractor. They told us we should be working.' Maksim looked away and shook his head. 'I was ten when I left here, but when I came back I was already thirty years old.'

He paused again, and the others around him used the pause to unleash their own histories. Few could remember the Civil War directly, but all knew the stories of how the Whites rode into the stanitsa and cut off people's heads, and how when the Reds rode in they did the same, and how the Greens who came next were no better. But the coming of the kolkhoz in 1933 was closer, and most recalled the men who brought it – town types with brutal faces who preserved their strength with pots of chicken and boiled fish while others starved. As children the Cossacks saw these men discussing their quotas and could not understand who these kulaks and hoarders were that they spoke of because everyone they knew lived off grass and water and was too weak to carry out their dead.

'We starved. We swelled up. We died.'

Tatyana Mikhailovna had a pale face circled by a cream kerchief. She spoke quietly. She had hidden up a tree when the first of them came and from there she had watched as they gathered the kulaks together. 'Of course they weren't proper kulaks, those ones. They were just people like us.'

They put them in a row. She counted eighteen. And one of the activists walked along behind them, shooting each one in the back of the head.

Two years later they came again. 'I was having lunch when I heard the bell going.'

Through the window she saw smoke coming out of the church. 'Mama! Mama!' she cried. 'The church is burning!'

Tatyana saw the tower melting, and then it was falling over like a candle. 'They said the priest had done it, and took him away –' She looked at me; the decades had done nothing to diminish her bewilderment. 'Do they think us fools? Why would a priest want to burn his own church?'

At the far end of the table sat Tatyana's husband. He was arm-wrestling. Bare-chested, he sat amidst a ring of cronies who watched and cheered as he and another locked hands. Tatyana eyed him from a distance, telling me quietly how eagerly he had joined the Cossack movement when it began a few years ago, and how each month he still went off with the others to the *krug*, while for her and her granddaughter life had just gone from bad to worse. He doted on his granddaughter, of course, would do anything for her – this slight figure who was sitting in the doorway of the hut. But where were they supposed to find money for medicine, and how could she tell her husband that his beloved girl, his little Anechka, was not well and only last week had attempted to commit suicide for the third time?

That night the singing went on late. I slept on the floor of one of the stanitsa's huts and in the morning left early. The air was still and the smoke rose in diaphanous steeples from the chimneys. High on the ridge was a great bald rock which thrust out through the side of the hill. I followed the path through sunny oak woods and a sward of pasture which curled around the rock's base. The sides of the rock were sheer on three sides and from its summit could be seen the mountains to the south, their peaks porcelain-white with snow.

During the Caucasian wars of the nineteenth century a certain Adygei horseman, rather than be captured by the Russians who were chasing him, rode over this rock to his death. The story had been told to me in the stanitsa with great glee – not because it concerned the death of an enemy but because it was such a splendid thing to have done. In general, in the Caucasian wars the Cossacks showed a lot more respect for their enemy than for the Russian regulars who came south to help.

Dropping down from the ridge, I crossed the river and came into the next stanitsa from the back. There I met a man named Igor Vasiliyevich who was sitting in his garden, both hands resting on his knees, watching a pair of hollyhocks. He fetched another chair and we both sat watching the hollyhocks.

'I remember the last real ataman we had when I was a boy. One hundred and fifteen he was, but he could still ride a horse like a young one.' The ataman had served in the private guard of Tsar Aleksandr III, and had once come up to Igor and twisted his ear for being a rascal. 'He was that kind of man. If he'd said he was the tsar himself, I'd have believed him.'

Igor shook his head and smiled at the memory, and then he said, 'Wish my Lusha was here. She'd have told you some stories.'

His Lusha had died two years earlier. They had been married forty years and the morning after her funeral he didn't know what to do. He sat in their room with his hands on his knees and stared up at the hand-tinted wedding photograph. 'After two days of that, I said to myself: "Igor Vassiliyevich, you can't sleep on the stove all your days!"'

So he left the stanitsa and walked. He walked for a long time and on the coast he joined a tour group in order to leave the country. After four and a half months he came to Jerusalem. When he got there he wasn't at all sure what to do. There were Mussulmen everywhere and no one spoke Russian. But he found the Russian church in the Garden of Gethsemane and the convent on the Mount of Olives. He stayed in the convent a long time, praying for his wife every day. When he'd done all his praying, he left the Holy City. It was another five months before he stepped into his stanitsa again. The whole journey had taken a year. But he felt better for having done it, much better.

'Look, I'll show you.' Igor stood and led me into his house. There were just two rooms and a large brick stove built into the wall between them. The windows and all the tables and the pillows on his wife's empty bed were covered in the most elaborate lace. 'That's Lusha's work. It's what she liked to do, that lacework.'

He pointed at a tourist poster of Jerusalem, taken from the Mount of Olives. We stood in front of it for some moments. Then he pointed and said: 'In this church here, there are seventy-seven faiths who worship all together. Christians all together and no Mussulmen. Isn't that beautiful!'

'Beautiful,' I agreed. But his finger was pointing not at a church, but at the Muslim shrine of the Dome of the Rock. I did not have the heart to correct him.

Sasha was a young agricultural engineer who lived in the stanitsa and was driving to Stavropol to see his fiancée. He said he could give me a lift. But by the time we left it was already late, and at some point beyond Labinsk Sasha scratched his chin and said we ought to find somewhere for the night.

'We will go to Urmikha.'

Urmikha was a small village where he used to spend summers as a student. He had a friend there called Gennady whom he hadn't seen for some years. The two of them, he said, used to get into all sorts of scrapes, and as we entered the village, crawling behind a press of byre-bound cows, he told the story of a trip they once took to the Urals.

They were in a small station, waiting for the Perm train, drinking *samogon* and fooling around. Being the time of Gorbachev's prohibition, the two policemen who pitched up at the station before the train did arrested Gennady and Sasha and threw them in the cells. There a number of other policemen beat them and robbed them. In the early hours they took pity on Gennady and Sasha and said they'd drive them to Perm. They drove for some time and then the policemen pointed at a glow of lights in the distance and said: 'Perm. You'd better start walking.'

They walked quickly as it was very cold and they had lost most of their clothes. The edge of Perm came closer. But when they reached it they found it was not Perm, but a secret military installation, ringed by barbed wire. Armed guards threatened to arrest them if they did not leave. It was dawn before they came to a village. There they were given shelter and food and clothes. The villagers gave them money too for the return trip.

'In our country,' said Sasha, 'you can always come across kind people.'

But Gennady was no longer in Urmikha. We found his mother. She lived alone in a small homestead and she was just closing the barn doors for the night. Two pails of milk stood next to her.

'Yes, I remember you, Sasha. It's been a long time.'

'Ten years.'

'Ten years.' Gennady's mother shook her head. 'Well, everything's different now. When you knew Gennady he was a boy with the sun in his face. But now he's drinking. He comes back and sits at the kitchen table and weeps all the time. His wife's a Jehovah's Witness. He's not really a man any more.'

She gave us his new address; then, bending to pick up the milk-pails, she turned to cross the yard.

Back on the steppe, it was already dark. The road cut through an expanse of rye fields which glowed in the moonlight. We drove for an hour or more. At the checkpoints on the main road, the police questioned us at length. It was almost midnight when we pulled up in front of a small apartment block. Several men were sitting outside in the heat.

'Is there a Gennady that lives here?' we asked.

'There certainly is.'

'Is he at home?'

'He just came in, drunk again.'

Gennady was sitting in his kitchen in a shirt unbuttoned to the waist. Sweat shone on the cliff of his forehead. He was very pleased to see Sasha and hugged him. Soon the table was covered with bowls of vegetables, and fish and vodka.

The missing years filled the pages of a floral-covered photo album. Gennady flicked through it with the drinker's false excitement; Sasha did no more than nod in response to the first wife, their child, a job in Astrakhan, then the first of the Cossack parades and the meetings and the new uniform. This uniform Gennady went to retrieve from the next room. He put it on – a tight brown astrakhan hat and a pale green *cherkesska* with a row of faux charges below the shoulder.

'Cost me a month's salary, Sash – but look at these seams!'

For a moment he stood before us – reborn Cossack of the old host, bold swaggering Cossack of the Caucasian Line, fearless border-sealing Cossack. Then he took the coat off. 'Sash, it's no good any more. Nothing's any good any more.'

Gennady had left the movement when he found out that the ataman had served sixteen years for rape.

*   *   *

Morning pressed its light upon the mess of Gennady's flat. Near Stavropol, I watched Sasha's car head into the traffic. I caught a bus and headed east again, aiming for that narrow gap in the Caucasus that is the Georgian Military Highway.

But first, there was a little rest and recreation in the town of Kislovodsk.

A Short History of Vodka

Kislovodsk is a spa town. It owes its entire existence to a few clefts in the rock from which bursts a carbonated water with the metallic taste of blood. An old Cossack I met there laughed when he told me how his great-great-grandfather used to board over those clefts to stop his cattle falling in. But once they had tamed the region's belligerent tribes, the Russians took over the local belief that the water held in its bubbles efficacious properties, able to prolong life and palliate gonorrhoea.

In its mountain setting, the spa became a potent mix of health and idle passions. The railway brought to Kislovodsk stern-faced industrialists from the cities of the north. They came in black suits with women encumbered by skirts who spun their parasols and stole glances at the mountain men. Pale daughters were paraded in the hope of catching the eye of some furloughed officer, firm-stepped from months of fighting along the cordon.

And the springs themselves, around which the town revolved, began to take on their own dandyish attire, dressed up like Ottoman *kiosques*, Gothick galleries and Hindu temples, and each day then and each day since has begun with a line of stooping supplicants waiting at these buildings with cups and plastic bottles for the arrival of the hieratic matrons, white-coated, commanding women preceded by a jailer's jangle of keys.

Everyone was sick in Kislovodsk – or at least everyone was

under the illusion that they could feel better. Despite the Soviet emphasis on reason, health in Russia has never really left the arena of blind faith, and there were times when the town appeared to me as little more than the headquarters of some elaborate cult. Along its cobbled alleys, vendors presided over trestle tables heavy with cures – herbal ointments, analgesics, antihistamines, expectorants, syringes, suppositories, herbstalks. On each bottle of local mineral water was listed the ailments it could treat: chronic gastritis (at high and normal acidities), gastric and duodenal ulcers, swollen lips, drooping testicles, cholecystitis, diabetes. Billboards advertised comedy shows as 'laughter cures'. Posters displayed a clamouring retinue of quacks and cranks. Pasted to lamp-posts, slapped onto bare walls were the saccharine smiles of men who guaranteed joy for the price of a few thousand roubles. One proposed perfect health through complete silence; another was peddling 'pure energy'; another claimed to be 'First Whole Person of 20th century'.

After months wandering around the steppe I was prepared to suspend my disbelief, to go along with the idea that Kislovodsk would restore me in some way. I found no difficulty in sinking into the town's lazy, convalescent rhythm, in ambling its flowery promenades, its wooded-glen parks. I took the waters – drank them, bathed in them, sat in their steam. I had my palm read, my bio-energy measured. I went to the casino and lost fifty dollars, went to the barber and had a shave, ate thinly-sliced *basturma* in the Intourist hotel, went to the casino again and won fifty dollars, and made sure at all times that I kept an eye on the peaks beyond the town, lest these spa pleasures distract me for too long from my meandering southward course.

In Kislovodsk, I rented a room from an elderly woman named Natalya Petrovna. She was fond of saying: 'They've drunk Russia away, you know, drunk it away . . .' She was also a great expert on local buses.

Natalya's working life had been spent as a teacher of ideology – 'People's Enlightenment' was the term she used. Her pension provided her with ten dollars a month, and the money I gave her would buy ice cream for her grandchildren when they came down to stay in July. They were good children, she said, a little unruly perhaps, and sometimes quite rude, but children nowadays – what can you do?

I slept on the balcony with rows of pickling jars and sprigs of drying tarragon. In the morning the sun fell through a canopy of fresh walnut leaves and filled the balcony with its light. I would listen to Natalya Petrovna tossing scraps of bread to the dogs in the yard: 'Maronchik! Sobachka!'

If it wasn't a holiday, she would spend the day working at her *dacha*, a small square of land which she reached by taking a no. 52 to the post office and waiting for a no. 10. It was very hot the week I was there and she came back exhausted each evening and lay with a compress on her legs. She brought bags of radishes. 'There's been no rain and that's why they're small – but they're spicier like that.'

Natalya Petrovna had two sons, two fun-loving boys who smiled on the kitchen wall from a black-and-white photograph. They were standing together, loose-hipped and laughing; the point of Mount Elbrus rose behind them. They had gone to Afghanistan together. They had written long letters home. They had sent photographs of themselves in uniform. Natalya's sons had returned separately, each one in a box.

'They drank it all away,' she said. 'Those generals just drank the poor boys' lives away.'

After several days in Kislovodsk, I was glad to leave.

'Take the 38 bus out of the town. Then there will be a small bus to Utskeken, one of those hunchback buses, an old Kuban . . .'

Natalya Petrovna was not keen that I should go at all. The hills were full of bandits, she said, and they shoot and take people in the night. But after the ward torpor of Kislovodsk, I found the threat of bandits quite alluring.

Just out of town, I passed from Russia into the republic of Karachai-Cherkassia. I left the bus near Utskeken and struck out across a treeless expanse of summer pasture. The land dropped away, and all morning I followed a river through its steep-sided valley. Lammergeiers drifted in the clear sky. The grass was spongy underfoot and fresh. One slope was thick with hazel while the other was bare, dusty-soiled and scattered with thorn bushes. For some time I sat high up, watching a couple of Karachai on ponies chasing a rogue heifer; they beat it with a long stick, threw a lasso at it, missed. They splashed and resplashed across the river, kicked the ponies up the slopes, then lost the little beast in the trees. They caught it only when it became fed up with running and stopped to graze beside the river.

Midday and the brightest hours I saw out beneath an ash tree. I read and slept and then the light thickened and a warm breeze came up the valley. In the late afternoon, I crossed the border back into Russia.

An abandoned pumping station lay beside a lake. In the trees was a deep-rutted track and across the ruts was slumped the figure of a man. I thought he was dead. A child came and squatted down beside him. 'Grandfather! Grandfather!'

The body grunted.

'Come home, Grandfather, we all love you!'

'Nobody loves me.'

'We all love you!'

The child saw me and ran away and the old man peered in

my direction. He blinked and focused his eyes. 'What sort are you?'

'A foreigner.'

'Don't make fun of me.' He lay there, muttering: 'See how they all make fun of me.' Then he raised one arm towards the sky and let out a great anguished moan which petered out in a tearful stream of invective. 'I'm an idiot! A fool! A jackass! The devil take me –'

Around the corner came a horse and cart and the man driving tutted and shook his head: 'Mikhail Stepanovich, not again!' I helped haul him onto the cart and one of his legs flopped down over the axle and we put it up and the cart headed off into the forest.

I carried on down the valley.

'Drinking is the joy of the Russes. We cannot do without it.'

With these words, in the tenth century, Prince Vladimir explained why his people would never accept Islam and why, therefore, Christianity was to be the state religion of Russia. He was not to know that this joy would a thousand years later leave his country with the world's highest per capita alcohol consumption, and that for each Russian man, a bottle of vodka would be consumed every two days.

But in the time of Prince Vladimir, there was no vodka. There was *syta* (mead) and *vino* and *kvass* and *beryozovitsa* (birch-sap wine). The art of distilling arrived in Russia in the same way as gunpowder and venereal disease, through contacts with the West.

In 1386 a Genoese legation brought to Moscow some flasks of what they called *'aqua vitae'*. The colourless liquid so astonished the Russians with its strength that at first it was considered suitable only for medicinal use. But before long there appeared in a Russian dictionary the entry for a hybridised English expression: *'Gimi drenki okoviten.'*

The state soon learned the fortuitous link between control of its people and control of alcohol. By establishing a monopoly on distilled liquor, tax revenues rose. The more that was drunk, the more tax came in. During much of the nineteenth century, with costly wars on numerous fronts, levies on alcohol accounted for 40 per cent of public income. Abandoning the state monopoly was a gesture available only to the most powerful Russian leaders – Peter I, Catherine II and Nicholas I. Likewise the occasional attempt at prohibition was always characteristic of a regime that had lost its way. Nicholas II tried it in 1914. The Bolsheviks continued the ban through their first chaotic years, and only in 1926 did they feel the confidence to relax it. But the most disastrous of all prohibitions was Gorbachev's.

In 1985, when vineyards were ripped up and vodka production reduced to a minimum, Soviet drinkers resorted to the well-developed practice of improvisation. Varnish, glue, window cleaner and brake fluid were all used. Toothpaste, taken in sufficient quantities, was found to produce an effect not unlike vodka, but only because of its toxins. Buying eau de cologne – dubbed 'the drink of intellectuals' – was prohibited before 2 p.m., and limited to two bottles per person. Storekeepers watched nonchalantly while desperate shoppers downed bottles of hair tonic at the counter.

The roots of such innovative drinking lay in the 1970s, when the contents of medicine cabinets and cleaning cupboards began to reveal unexpected properties. The greatest chronicler of this reckless cult was Venedikt Erofeev, who believed drinking to be the only true method of self-expression available to Soviet man, the only honest act in a dishonest world. In his *Moscow to the End of the Line* he gives a connoisseur's guide to cocktails with names like 'Jordan's Waters' or 'Lenin's Lady'. 'Balsam of Canaan' he suggested making with methylated spirits, Velvet beer and furniture polish. 'Bitches' Brew' ('a beverage which overshadows all others') was a combination of Zhiguli beer, Sadko shampoo, dandruff treatment, athlete's foot remedy and small-bug killer. 'Tear of a Komsomol Girl', a blend of various fragrant cosmetics (including lavender toilet water and nail polish), depended for its effect on the precise manner of stirring – to be conducted strictly with a sprig of honeysuckle: 'I simply die laughing when I see someone stirring a "Tear" with dodder.'

In a guide book, I came across various recipes for intoxication developed during Gorbachev's ban:

1 Put black polish on a slice of bread. Leave overnight. In morning, remove excess polish and it's ready to eat.
2 Mix glue or toothpaste with water, filter out and drink.
3 Soak white bread with eau de cologne.
4 Boil one wooden table leg with sugar and water, collect the vapours. Tastes like vodka.
5 Shave a part of your head the size of a coin, apply black shoe polish. Cover whole head, except the part shaved. Go for a walk in the sun.

In the second year of Gorbachev's ban, eleven thousand Soviet citizens died from such adventuring – a figure comparable to the toll for the entire Afghan war.

The shadows rose higher up the valley's slopes. A yellow evening light settled on the open ground. Some time later, I reached a spring and there came across another old man. With his white beard and crumpled *muzhik* smock, he looked like Tolstoy in his peasant phase. Beside him on a rock was a canvas backpack.

'A companion,' he said, and we fell into step.

'You have been collecting?' he asked.

'Just walking. You?'

'I was collecting grass.'

Out of the top of his pack he pulled a bundle of hazel twigs tied with ribbons of grass. His pack was full of these bundles – twigs and flowers and grasses – each one meticulously tied. At random he pulled them out, running them under his nose: 'Lungs . . . this one, stomach . . . ague . . . wounds.'

His face was shaded and graded and contoured like a mountain-map. He trod that thin line between sage and charlatan, and as we walked I was constantly revising my opinion as to which one he really was.

'I know three hundred grasses. People come to me and I look at them and give them a tea.'

'Just by looking?'

'By looking only. I learnt from my grandfather in Belorussia, and he from his.'

'Can you see anything wrong with me?'

He stopped in the road and passed the flat of his hand down in front of my chest and stomach.

'Nothing.'

'Nothing?'

'A little liver, here, perhaps . . .'

We walked on for a few minutes and then he said suddenly: 'But your country has a bad fate, you know.'

'Oh?'

'Its heart is failing and it will die.'

'What about Russia?'

'Russia? Russia has poisoned herself! She will fall. And when Russia falls, she will take many with her.'

*   *   *

I returned that night to Kislovodsk. I had hoped to reach a certain village in the mountains, but the southern evenings were quick to come and the comforts of Kislovodsk occupied me for one last night.

Only the Malformed Need Wear Clothes

It was a Cossack of the Terek *voisko* who told me about it first. He lived in the top room of one of Kislovodsk's old hillside villas. He was sitting in full uniform, on a wooden chair in the middle of his bare wooden floor, talking of the acrobatic things he used to do on his horse. His horse was called Larisa ('Like my mother') and she was a Hasaut horse.

'Hasaut?'

'It's a village. In the mountains. There's Abaza people who live there. Fiery people they are, and devilish fighters.' (The Abaza were scions of the Abkhaz who some five hundred years ago had drifted eastwards, away from the Black Sea.)

'It's a magic place,' continued the Cossack, 'on account of an energy line they call the *shambola*.' The same line had been found in the Himalayas and was said to run through the village; in the Himalayas on this line was found the yeti; the Cossack said that Hasaut also had its beast.

As a Terek Cossack of long tradition, such things would have been beneath his mentioning – mountain lore, the stuff of pagan tribesmen. But Hasaut was worthy of his respect for one reason and one reason only: its people had always bred the finest horses in the region.

It was not an easy place to get to. 'Go to Kichi-Balyk,' he

said. 'You might find someone going to Hasaut from there. Or you might not.'

Kichi-Balyk was a small village high above Kislovodsk, at the far end of the bus route. It was not much of a village. But in a yard behind the old kolkhoz building I found a Kamaz lorry full of sheep-shearers, and they were going up to Hasaut for the shearing.

It was a beautiful morning. The sheep-shearers stood with me in the back, gripping the load-boards. They were silent, leathery-faced men who spent the journey passing around a lump of cheese. An overnight mist had lodged in the valleys and the sun was just rising above the mountains, tracing the contours with its shadows. Higher up, the trees gave way to a series of round-backed hills and beyond them was an endless row of blue-green ridges.

The road reached its summit, and in the distance rose the snowy peak of Elbrus. Then the land fell away and the lorry gave a sudden downwards lurch. The sheep-shearers fell against each other and one of them dropped the cheese. Here the rock had been dynamited to create an impossible series of short switchback bends. The wheels of the Kamaz slid on the corners, pitching gravel over the edge. The cliff ended and the road straightened out and spread below was a lost world of a valley. At one end was the village of Hasaut – the walls of its corrals a grid of symmetry in the higgledy-piggledy of rocky outcrops. Above the village was a V of land where two rivers merged. There was no other habitation in the valley. Only as we drew nearer did Hasaut reveal itself for what it really was – a ghost town. I had not expected this. Its houses were roofless, its rocky streets flanked by broken walls. Only in places was there an inhabited house. It looked like an elevated Pompeii.

The shearers set about their shearing and I headed out through the calf-high lines of collapsed walls in search of a woman called Tamara. I found her scattering seed to a squeaking horde of chicks. Upturned jars stood over her fence-posts, and she greeted me with a casual weariness. She lived alone.

'The warm days are not far now.' She bent to place a bowl of *smetana* on the table. We were sitting on logs outside her door. I asked about the ruins.

'Before, there were eight hundred households.'

'And now?'

'Maybe sixteen.' She spooned out the *smetana*. 'In the twenties they left for Turkey and for the towns. Then they left for prison and the north. In the war they left with the Germans.'

Once people left Hasaut they did not come back. The thresholds of their houses grew thick with grass and after the second winter or maybe the third, the uncleared snow proved too much for the roofs and they would buckle under its weight. Then the villagers, the ones who remained, would take the stones and use them to rebuild their own walls or to make stockades for their beasts.

'And then there were the deportations.'

The deportations. In 1943, suffering from the potentate's affliction – the fear-driven cycle of dissent and retribution, dissent and retribution – Stalin had ordered the cleaning-up of his empire's southern provinces. Chechens, Karachai, Balkars, Ingush and Tatars had all, in his eyes, not resisted the Germans quite as vigorously as they might. With a flourish of his Party chairman's signature he authorised the forcible removal of more than two million people. At a time when the war had just begun to turn in his favour, Stalin chose to deploy thousands of troops and hundreds of trains on these cathartic duties. He was right to question the loyalty of these people; his own policies were catching up with him.

'It was like in a dream. We had no warning. They came with trucks and took everyone. I do not know one person who was not taken. My grandmother couldn't move and we said to the soldiers: 'Look, she cannot move. She is 110 years old.' They made us take her. There was another woman who was 116 and she too had to go. Six days in a wagon and there was snow on the ground when we arrived. We planted beetroot and were hungry all those years. My grandmother died. I had six sisters and they all died. I don't even want to remember.'

Tamara stood. The chicks fled before her. She went into the hut and came out again with a black-and-white photograph. 'This is how it was before.'

The photograph was taken looking down the valley – the same bare slopes, the same flat-topped cliffs, the same spurs. In the foreground stood a group of men in flared sheepskin coats, tied at the waist, and unkempt sheepskin hats. Beyond this group was a stubby minaret and part of a large building with bulbous cupolas topped with crescent moons. This, said Tamara, was her grandfather's house. There is no trace of it now and only the outside walls of the mosque remain.

I turned the photograph over to see the date. 1929. The year when the honeymoon with Stalin ended, when the diversity of the old empire's rural communities began to be destroyed. The photograph was poignant beyond words.

On the back of it was also a sticker which read:

> Prudence Cuming Associates Ltd
> 28–29 Dover St
> London W1X 3PA

'Where did you get this?' I asked.
'What?'
'The photograph – where did it come from?'
'A man came some years ago. His father had taken it.'
Of course: Daniel Farson. He had retraced the route that his father, Negley Farson, had taken in 1929. I remembered

there'd been a Caucasian village, but not that it was Hasaut.

She smiled. 'You find the photograph interesting, I think.'

'Yes, I do.'

Negley Farson spent a year in the Soviet Union, between September 1928 and September 1929. Not until 1951 did he publish his account of it, *Caucasian Journey*. By that time the late twenties appeared as:

> unquestionably the high point of the Russian Revolution. Never since has the dream of 1917, of the Old Bolsheviki, looked so near to being realised. The Russians were still human (as they will be again some day). You could still travel about Russia and talk to strange people without their being terrified.

It was an exciting time to be in Moscow particularly, one of those brief moments in history when ideas and action appeared to be synchronised. Thus he reports the group of 'startlingly beautiful young girls' who boarded a tram wearing nothing but a ribbon around their midriffs with the legend 'ONLY THE MALFORMED NEED WEAR CLOTHES'.

To fellow-travellers, as well as to Farson, the twenties were good years. The turmoil of the Revolution and Civil War had settled. Prosperity was only another dam, another steelworks away. Then came the First Five-Year Plan, the consolidation of Stalin as leader, the campaign against the kulaks, collectivisation, the purges, and the fine dream of Lenin and the 'Old Bolsheviki' was shattered.

It now looks a little different. Far from being a time of hope, the twenties appear with hindsight to be merely a breathing space. While the bold exponents of the avant-garde rode naked on tramcars, while the fellow-travellers travelled hopefully, while the peasants built up their herds and made use of tracts of redistributed land, the hounds of real Leninism were waiting to be unleashed. Post-Soviet revisionists have debunked the myth of the good Lenin. Archives have revealed him to be, during his short time in power, easily a match for Stalin in terms of ruthlessness. Stalin did not corrupt Lenin's high ideas. He was simply able to put them into action.

Just below Tamara's house was a small plot, fenced off by steel railings. In each corner were ornate little finials. Five zinc-painted headstones stood inside the railings.

One morning in the summer of 1937, five Party activists arrived in the village. Everyone knew why they were there. Quotas had been issued to the District Committees: so many to the camps, so many to be eliminated. Hasaut's dissenters took to the hills. On a moonless night, a group of them rode back into the village. They went to the houses of the activists. They took them to the edge of the village. They shot the activists, then rode back into the hills.

A unit of the Red Army was sent to the mountains to flush out these bandits, and although the Reds were ambushed and harried and beaten back, they did manage to conduct savage reprisals in the village of Hasaut. It is no surprise that the arrival of the Wehrmacht five years later should have been greeted with such relief.

I leaned on the railings and looked at the plot. The sun had fallen behind the mountains and the air was cold. It was strange, in this village of ruins, that the grave was so well kept-up – the railings intact and freshly painted. Strange too that such care should be taken over the bodies of the villagers' sworn enemies. But after all the Soviet decades – with their beatings and fleeings, their tight-lipped resistance and mass deportations – this fenced-off square of mountain turf was just a grave, and graves are graves and should not be trodden by man nor beast.

*   *   *

The sheep-shearers had been billeted in the old schoolroom. I joined them there for the night. Their hands were blackened with sheep oil. They ate sheep and slept under sheepskin blankets. Some of them even looked like sheep. When, sitting round the fire, I mentioned the *shambola*, they muttered and scoffed and were silent.

But then one of them said how his cousin had seen the beast, and after that somehow they all found stories of lights in the sky, strange occurrences and sightings of a dark and shambling creature which alone of the mountain-dwellers had managed to escape the deportations.

Puppets for Peace

In the town of Karachayevsk, it had just rained. Smoky patches of mist hung against the mountainside; the streets were running with water. Where the bus stopped three dripping cows stood on the pavement and a *shashlik*-vendor lay asleep under a tarpaulin. The faint roar in the distance was the upper Kuban.

Two things had brought me to Karachayevsk, and to begin with I drew a blank with each. Wandering around the sodden backstreets, eyes raised to the hills, I failed to pick out the Alan church that stood above the town. But a woman armed with her 'just-in-case' string bag did manage to help me with my other quest, and pointed to a rain-streaked housing-block.

Ashod Balayan opened the door of his tenth-storey flat. His beard was thicker than before and a little whiter. His smile was just the same.

'Oh, this happy life!' He clutched my hand.

Two years earlier in Yerevan, in that blacked-out and besieged city, I had spent some time with Ashod and a group of other painters. There his enthusiasm had been so striking that I'd ended up feeling quite worried for him. Now in Karachayevsk I could see it remained undimmed. He was here for the summer, painting and collaborating on a dozen different projects.

His flat had two rooms. One he used for his work in oils and the other, in which he slept, was put aside for all other work. He had written a children's story of beautiful simplicity. Beside his bed was a Russian translation of the *Kon-Tiki* book and a pamphlet with the title 'What we do not Know'. On a large board were laid out the models for a forthcoming puppet show in Paris entitled *PUPPETS FOR PEACE!*

Ashod turned from one thing to the next, pointing to this, explaining that – the markings on a world map, the significance of an abacus hung above his bed, a dried flower, all part of some grand scheme he had no time at present to consider. He loved his work, and his love made it plausible.

I pointed to a diagram of concentric broken circles; on it was scribbled a great number of notes.

'That is Ratan-600.'

Ashod's uncle had been one of the great Soviet astronomers. During his career he had discovered a total of fifteen hundred galaxies. Ratan-600, a vast radio telescope near Karachayevsk, had enabled him to do so. When Ashod was twenty he had gone up to these mountains to see his uncle and sat in on a conference of astrophysicists.

'I didn't understand one word of what they were saying. But I looked at this diagram – it was in a slide-show – and suddenly I saw it. It's supposed to be a drawing of the mutual properties of an atom, a galaxy and a solar system. But I looked at it and I saw my own life! All our lives! You see?'

'No.'

'Well, we all start here, from the centre, and try to find the outer rim – that is understanding. The scientist swims there, through all his analysis. But the artist must jump – must leap! If the artist tries to use analysis he will fall; if the scientist jumps he will drown. You see?'

'I think so.'

Ashod steepled his hands. 'Look at it like this. The artist's jump is like humour, like laughter – a sudden leap to meaning.

Analysis kills the joke. And if an artist cannot laugh, he is nothing.'

One thing above all now dominated Ashod's work. Several years ago, in his studio in Yerevan, he had become suddenly struck by a strange and powerful presence. It was the number twelve. Since then he had been able to paint only twelve – groups of twelve people, the apostles, the number itself. He had subsequently added the first four letters of the Armenian alphabet to his repertoire, and these too now peppered his canvases. But twelve remained for him nothing less than the manifestation of his life.

'Why twelve, Ashod?'

He shrugged. 'Really, I don't know. And I don't want to! When people think they have answers at once they try and make the world a better place. And look at what that has meant in this country! No, the world to me is a question which we must spend our life thinking about. A great big wonderful question! There is only one real answer – and that is death.'

I left Ashod in the early afternoon. From the street I looked back and saw him standing on his balcony. He was gripping the balustrade with one hand and waving with the other. I had the impression that were he to loosen his grip on that balustrade, he would rise up over the rooftops of Karachayevsk, drift away across the Caucasus and disappear into the blue somewhere above his native Armenia.

Ashod knew about the Alan church, and pointed down the valley to the village of Kosta Hetagurovo. Above the village, he said, there you'll see your church. The rain had cleared and the afternoon was warm. Deep flood-gullies sliced through the yellow clay of the hill. A drovers' track led up from the village to a low saddle and there was the church, a neat little edifice built straight up out of the rock. But for a gliding eagle, the place was deserted. A sign read, in Russian: '*Built by Greek masters for the Alans in IX–Xth centuries. Destroyed by Soviet powers in the 1920s. Renovated by the youth of Kosta Hetagurovo in 1994.*'

The Alans. Everyone down here had their own ideas about the Alans. Somewhere beneath the theories and the facts, the linguistics and the archaeology, the written accounts, lay the flesh and blood of another vanished steppe people. The Alans were a sub-group of the bellicose Sarmatians. No sight was more shameful to the Alans than an old male who had failed to die in battle. They drank mares' milk and ate horseflesh and some groups swaddled their children so tightly the head took on the shape of an egg. Others seared the right breast of their daughters so that they could draw a bow in battle; virgins were required to kill before they could marry. The early Alans worshipped the image of a sword thrust into the bare earth, a cult which may well have been the source for Excalibur in the Arthurian cycles.

Ptolemy linked them with the Scythians – the 'Alani-Scythae' he called them – and has them coming out of Central Asia to settle to the west of the Don. When in the early Christian centuries the Alans were scattered by the Hunnic invasions, they revealed a remarkable capacity to reappear in far-off places.

At the Battle of Hastings, for instance. On one of the Norman flanks a group of cavalry, suddenly faced by a mass of English troops, turned its horses and fled. The English broke their lines and gave chase – whereupon the Norman cavalry turned again and slaughtered the lot of them. It was a decisive moment in the battle. The feigned retreat was favoured by the Alans, as it had been by the Scythians. The cavalry at Hastings was commanded by a Count Alan, and in Normandy the word '*allain*' was long used for a man of wild temperament.

By the time of Hastings, the Alans had already been in western

Europe a thousand years. The Roman Emperor Hadrian had written a poem in praise of an Alan horse: 'Borysthenes the Alan was Caesar's horse . . . saliva sprinkled from his mouth to the end of his tail in the chase.' Five and a half thousand Alan horsemen were sent by Marcus Aurelius for duty on Hadrian's Wall. Both Alan-bred horses and Alan-bred dogs were famed in Europe; in Spain, two Alan hounds appear on the coat of arms of the town of Alano. Chaucer wrote of the ferocious Alan wolf-hound.

And this group of steppe warriors has left its mark not only in ancient chronicles, but with every man named Alan or Alain, every family named Allen. In northern Italy there are old Alan settlements: Alagna and Allegno and Alano di Piave. In France dozens more: Alançon, Alaincourt (five of them), Courtalain, Alaniers, Allainville . . . In Eastern Europe, the names Serbia and Croatia come not from Slavonic roots but from Alan tribes. In Poland, the entire noble class, the *szlachta*, claimed a some-what tenuous descent from the Alans, and their heraldry is peppered with symbols matched to Sarmatian and Alan archae-ological finds.

The Alans spread east as well as west. William of Rubruck, en route to Mongolia, came across them in the Urals. Thirty thousand were recorded in 1318 living on the Chinese coast. At the same time De Marignolli found them a significant presence in the Mongol empire, and calls them 'the greatest and noblest nation in the world, the bravest and fairest of men'. To them he attributed much of Genghis's success in battle. In a letter to the Pope, the Great Khan refers to the Alans as 'our servants and his Christian sons'.

For many centuries, the greater part of the North Caucasus was known as Alania. The Alans married into the Georgian royal family and into the great Macedonian dynasty of Byzantium, but after the Mongol invasions they disappeared. Alania and the

Alans are long since forgotten by their descendants in the cramped coastal villages of China, the turfy green valleys of Lancashire, the inlets of Brittany and the castellated villages of Spain.

The church was cool inside and dark. The floor was a fine earthy dust and there was just the sound of the wind rising and falling through the empty windows. In them was framed a section of the valley's far slope, rock and forest and a corner of sky. I imagined no one had been up here for weeks.

A shuffling noise made me spin round. In the shadows was a series of tiny lights. They darted and bobbed. They flashed and blinked. Then they bleated. Their mass of grey, woolly forms had bunched up, each one struggling to get further into the apse.

So, no Alans here. Only in one part of the Caucasus does any trace of them remain, where they speak a version of the old Sarmatian tongue, and where in the modern manner their Alan roots, ignored and unknown for centuries, had suddenly become more talked about than all the recent batterings of the Soviet years. These people were in a way the only true heirs of the ancient dwellers of the steppe – certainly more legitimate than the Cossacks. They were the Ossetians, now confined to a pair of mountain republics which straddled the Caucasian ridge, two hundred miles to the east.

They shook their heads on the bus. They pointed at the plains: 'Look, how dry it is!'

It was June and the fields were already harvest-yellow. The sky was cloudless, a pale and distant blue, and the heat from the earth set the horizon rippling like water.

'Down here,' they said, 'it is three weeks since it rained and even then it was only two drops more than nothing.'

In Vladikavkaz, capital of the autonomous republic of North

Ossetia, it was a different story. The mountains rose straight out of the town. Clouds rose straight out of the mountains and in the mid-afternoon they thickened into a thundery mass. Searching for the Institute of Ossetian Studies, I watched the first coin-size spots appear on the pavement. Then it began in earnest. Women scuttled into doorways with handbags over their heads; dogs ran flat-furred through the water. The Terek river, which I crossed more often than necessary, filled. The streets filled. Soon it was hard to tell between them.

The institute was at the top of a marble staircase. In the offices there was not a great deal going on – some sitting, some smoking, a little personal shoe-inspecting. I stood in the doorway while water from my clothes dripped onto the floor.

'*Don.*' One of the women pointed at the small puddle that had formed.

'Yes, I'm sorry.'

'No – in Alan language, the word for water is "*don*".'

Clearly I'd come to the right place for the Alans.

She continued: 'Is there not a river in the north of your country named Don?'

'Yes.'

'From the Alan soldiers on Hadrian's Wall.'

'And the Russian Don?'

'An Alan name.' She raised a rhetorical-looking finger. 'Am I right in thinking that there is with you a place called Croy-don?'

'An Alan town?'

'It means "mill on the water".'

'And Lon-don,' another put in. 'It means "dirty water".'

A little later there appeared a man they described as the world's leading Alan scholar. Not Ossetian himself but Russian, Professor Kuznyetsov showed me into his office, telling me not to take too seriously the toponymic enthusiasm of his colleagues.

Every month the professor came up to Vladikavkaz on the

train from Mineral'nye Vody. He had swept-back hair and bright, open eyes. He explained the origin of the name 'Ossetian' – from the Georgian name for the Alans, '*Owsni*', thence to the Russian '*Osetiny*'. He smiled when he discussed the importance of the stag in Ossetian heraldry, and his gap-teeth showed like outstretched fingers. His office was very small and there was hardly room for the bookshelves and the desk and the two chairs. Yet in the corner was a very narrow bed where, in the ascetic dedication to his trade, the professor slept for one week in every four.

Briefed by Kuznyetsov, I took a bus up into the Ossetian mountains. Some valleys were waisted so tightly it was like being in a cave. In others, the slopes were set back, rising in giant steps to the peaks. It rained continuously. Water dropped in narrow cords from the overhanging rocks. The rivers rose; mist hid the mountains.

Wherever you turned in these valleys there were stone-built towers. Topping ridges, in clusters around the settlements, the towers were the refuge of the last of the Alans. Chased into the mountains by the Mongols, the once fearless Alans were forced to build these defensive towers. When marauders ventured into the valleys, beacons were lit from the watchtowers, which in turn were seen from others, and soon everyone would know of the marauding. The villagers would then retreat into their own towers, pull in the ladder and live off stores. The attackers camped outside. Whoever had the best supplies was the victor.

The towers were remarkable structures. Some of the basalt blocks were the size of a small cow, yet the sides were smooth as they tapered towards the top. High above the main valley, I reached a deserted village of them. Boulders surrounded the towers' stumpy ruins. Only one dwelling was inhabited. A man in a fur hat was standing on the sheet of bedrock that was his yard. He was looking down into the valley through a pair of military binoculars.

'I like to watch their life down there. Sometimes you see something move.'

His wife hobbled along the verandah and leaned on the parapet. Her face seemed set in a permanent wince.

'It's her allergies,' he explained.

Two years before, they had moved up from the Ardon valley. She'd been ill there and here the mountain air was better. But she was still ill and now they could go no higher.

The rain fell harder. The man put down his binoculars and scowled at the grey cushion of cloud; the streams were filling and his sheep were in need of collection. As I left the village I could see him darting up over the fallen blocks of stone, past the strange beehive huts of the dead, into the mist. His wife stood unmoving on the verandah.

Down in the valley I came across a war memorial with a hundred names on it. An elderly villager was standing in front of it, picking his teeth. That a small town should have given so many to the Patriotic War struck me less than that the memorial was topped by a bust of Stalin.

'They tried to take him away,' said the old man. 'But we just put him back! He was one of ours.'

Stalin's mother was Georgian and she had married a man named Dzhugashvili, which was a Georgianised version of Dzhugaev. And the name Dzhugaev was itself a Russified version of an old Ossetian clan.

Another claim for the Alans. Serbia, Croatia, Croydon – now they could hold up Stalin as one of their sons.

But so what? Ethnicity is an arbitrary science. The chauvinism of these border regions only highlights its falsehoods. Go back four or five hundred years and the number of ancestors of any currently-living individual increases dramatically. At the same time the world's total population diminishes. The two figures converge at some point in the Middle Ages. Even given a large degree of duplication, it is quite possible that at the time of the Mongol invasions, when the Alans disappear from contemporary accounts, a great many of us have a common ancestor with Stalin.

Back down in Vladikavkaz, I prepared to cross into Georgia. But the hotel I was staying in had been commandeered by Russian troops. A military policeman sat with his feet up on the desk and everywhere were military packs and guns and soldiers.

'Try Yuri,' said the receptionist, above the barracks noise. 'Yuri lets out rooms.'

She scribbled down an address and as I left, a group of off-duty regulars let off a signal grenade from the balcony. I looked back to see the hotel veiled by blood-red smoke.

Yuri lived across the river. It had been nearly a year since the rest of his family had fled this troublesome region for the north, leaving him behind to sell the house for whatever he could. But I had the impression Yuri rather liked being a rarity, staying on, rattling around in his balconied villa on the banks of the Terek while he let out rooms to the ethnic flotsam of the Caucasus. They in turn, unlike his own people, were prepared to listen at least for a while to his drawn-out stories of the merchant navy.

He sat most of the time in his courtyard, alone, his squarish figure dappled beneath the vine. 'Welcome my house,' he said when I arrived. 'I am an English speaker.'

Indeed he was. It was an eccentric English sprinkled with aphorisms that he had found in 'great English books'. Yet on his bookshelves I could see only slightly risqué novels of the

1950s, with titles like *Tennis-Party Passion*, *Teenage Tearaway* and *Sports Car Cowboy*. He was proud of his collection of European souvenirs – 'the most beautiful cultural remembrances' – plaster-cast Greek statues, a picture of a car made out of watch parts and a shell-covered lampstand from Dieppe.

He showed me a room. 'It's clean, clean – all been cleaned! As Dickens said it is "clean like after a funeral". Is it satisfactory?'

'Yes, Yuri. Thank you.'

'Good.' He lingered in the doorway, searching for the *mot juste*. 'Here you will be calm, you will be happy – you will be by the seaside.'

One of Yuri's tenants was a student – an Ossetian – named Omar. Omar had very red hair. On his forearms it stood out like tiny clips of saffron. He had left his village and come to Vladikavkaz to study, but there he had found something even more compelling than civil engineering – Islam.

'Next year,' he said, 'I'll make the *haj*. I'll go to Jerusalem first – where Mohammed rose to Heaven. When he came back he said that he'd prayed there sitting between Moses and Christ. They asked him what Christ was like and he said he was the most beautiful man you've ever seen.'

'Your family is Christian?'

'Of course. I was brought up studying the Bible. But have you seen those Orthodox churches? So full of beauty – icons and all those things of brass. But there's no sense there, no sense at all.'

In his room, yards and yards of Koranic texts ran round the wall. A poster was pinned up with step-by-step instructions on how to pray. It reminded me of one of those lifesaving charts you see in public swimming baths. Omar left Yuri's the next day to meet a famous mullah from Daghestan.

That morning Yuri ambled into the courtyard doing up a tie of spectacular green stripes. He was going to visit his friend Maksim Ivanovich. 'Yes, yes, it is his birthday. Every year this day he massacres a chicken and we make as you say – a harvest feast. You will accompany me, if it is your wish.'

Maksim was not at home, so we went to the house of another of Yuri's friends, Igor.

'Where is Maksim Ivanich, Igor? He has a chicken.'

'No idea.'

We went to Gennady's house. Gennady was also Russian. He was sitting in his yard in a pair of pressed trousers and a hat of plastic straw. Yuri sat down. 'How is your mother?'

'I'm going out,' interrupted Gennady.

'Where to?'

'Funeral.'

'Do you know where Maksim Ivanich is?'

'No.'

So we left Gennady's house and went to the local government office. A Communist flag hung outside and inside three women were drinking tea. 'Where's Maksim?' he asked. 'Maksim Ivanich?'

Maksim, they said, had gone to live in Moscow.

'Oh.'

Back out on the street, the sound of thunder echoed from the south. 'Oh, well,' sighed Yuri. 'What is lost in time's pocket is God's wages. That is an old English expression.'

We tried the house of another friend, but he was ill.

'Let's go and see Valeri!'

But I had run out of time. I had to go to the Institute of Ossetian Studies.

'All right, then. You do your business.' He was standing by the road, the mountains a dark mass above him. 'I will find something to do. I am not running, I am not dancing, I am walking *piano*. Yes, yes ... But you, you must hurry. Run fast like a squirrel!'

*   *   *

The last night at Yuri's, I was awake at three. Outside the window I could see the tangle of poplar branches and an orange glow behind them. I was thinking about Tbilisi and the Georgian Military Highway and border posts when there was a sound – a single sharp sound like a car backfiring, or a shot. Then silence. I strained to hear anything else but there was nothing. Then it came again. It was a shot. I crossed to the window and could see the pools of light beneath the streetlamps. Everything was still. The stillness of Russian nights always amazed me; sometimes I felt like the last person alive. Then came another shot. Shouts this time – a wild shouting, not of someone injured but of someone afraid, an aggressor's shouts. It came from the yard opposite and was hidden from view. There were two more shots in quick succession and then three cars drove away, very fast – a Niva, a Mercedes and a BMW. Their brake-lights flashed briefly as they slowed to turn out of the street, and then they were away, off towards the bridge over the Terek. Silence again. Nothing moved. Only after a few minutes could I make out the very faint hissing of wind in the midsummer leaves. It began to rain.

In the morning no one knew a thing about it. The sun shone on the high sides of apartment blocks. Women were leaning from their windows, constructing bunting-lines of washing.

The bus to Tbilisi was full of people. The aisles were full of sacks, and the sacks were full of pig fat. On top of one of the sacks lay a brand-new satellite dish. There wasn't a spare inch of room anywhere. I squatted next to a man who balanced a baby daughter on my knee, her twin on his, and said: 'I speak five languages: Russian, Georgian, Armenian, Azerbaijani – and ours.'

'What's yours?'

'Assyrian.'

The bus pulled south out of Vladikavkaz and began to climb. The night's rain lay in great ponds and shone on the grass. Ahead the road ran into a gap in the cliffs where the Terek river came bubbling out. This was the Georgian Military Highway, the entrance to the Scythian Gates, what the Persians called the Dar-y-Al, the Gate of the Alans. For years I'd wanted to do this journey. I'd failed once, four years earlier. I hadn't even come close that time – without papers, without contacts, with an earthquake in Abkhazia and a war in South Ossetia, I'd been forced to go round the Caucasus by way of the Black Sea.

The Assyrian jabbed me in the ribs and said: 'You must look. The road is broken but the nature is nice.'

We passed through villages shell-scarred from the war with the Ingush; we passed through checkpoints, beside the broken hulls of gravel lorries, beneath bushes of hazel and beech that had somehow found root on bare rockfaces. The cliffs grew closer to each other. The road steepened. The military hardware at the checkpoints increased and then the guards were wearing helmets, sitting beside dug-in artillery, staring out of pillboxes, and the gorge itself became little more than a darkened alley.

At the Russian border, they came onto the bus, checking passports. Seeing mine, the guard flicked his head.

'Off.'

'What?'

'OFF!'

I handed the Assyrian his daughter and left the bus. The bus drove on. I crossed a wide-open stretch of concrete to the guardpost. The air was cool and a familiar cloak of cloud had cut out the sun. Carrion crows hopped around the waste ground.

The officer said the border was closed to foreigners. I waved official-looking letters at him and he said he'd call his superior in Moscow. I settled down to wait. With that unctuous attitude to authority bred by needing something, I befriended the guards.

One of them was a Terek Cossack with a bad case of toothache – I gave him several analgesics. He took them all at once. Within ten minutes he was smiling again. Within fifteen minutes he was whispering in my ear: 'When I give the word, you run across the border. OK? I promise I won't shoot.' Then he laughed. Then he was asleep.

Another of them squatted with me against the wall and, lighting a cigarette, recounted how his grandfather had been born in Palermo, went to Athens, married a Greek, had a daughter who'd gone to Georgia, then married a Russian and had a son. 'And here I am,' he exclaimed. 'A total international man.'

But neither of them could help me. Moscow said no. If I wanted to go to Georgia there was a perfectly good flight from Moscow. I was damned if I was going to go back to Moscow. The only other route across the Caucasus was the much smaller Ossetian Military Highway – and that led not into Georgia proper but the war-bound enclave of South Ossetia. Whether it was possible then to cross the front lines, I had no idea.

Pushkin and the Old People

There'd been a conference in Vladikavkaz and they were going home. They were going back over the mountains to South Ossetia in a bus which must already have been old when Stalin died. Archaeologists, ethnographers, demographers, all carrying on with the conference across the broken bench seats – pondering the unresolved questions around an early Sarmatian griffin torque, the survival of a curious phoneme in modern Ossetian, discussing plans for the re-establishment of the Via Alanica, the westward route of the Alans from the foothills of the Caucasus through the Ukraine, Hungary, Austria, Switzerland, France and from Spain into North Africa. No one could quite agree on the dimensions of a Koban funerary chamber which had recently been discovered, but that only meant the debate could go on longer: and these Ossetian academics well knew that a really good scholarly debate is measured not by its resolution, but by its duration.

'One hundred and fifteen,' said a philosopher. 'Maybe even more.'

Someone whistled.

The philosopher was head of South Ossetia's Committee for Jurisdiction and Human Rights and he was telling me of his grandfather. 'He of course had no idea how old he was, and he didn't care.'

'But you think he was 115?'

'That's what everyone said.'

Years earlier, doing a degree in the hit-and-miss discipline of anthropology, I'd come across an ethnography of the Caucasus's old people. I remember the picture of a woman strolling along ahead of a parade, smoking (110 years old); the man rearing on a horse (120); the twins of 119 and a great many others who were well into their second century. My initial reaction was: it's all nonsense, boastful exaggeration. And then, what is their secret?

According to the ethnographer, verification of age was easier than it sounds. By asking the 'long-livers' and other members of the community what age they were when certain things happened – a birth, a marriage, a natural disaster or war – he drew up a matrix of chronological figures that could be checked and double-checked against each other. In this way he arrived at a figure which, he claimed, would be out by no more than a couple of years.

As to how they lived so long, the ethnographer drew a blank. Just as no health fad is ever as deterministic as its followers would like to believe, so in this study the secret of longevity seemed to be that there was no secret. The only distinguishing feature of the long-living villagers that I could see was not their diet, or their water, or any strange exercise regime, but the fact that they'd lived in the same place for thousands of years. The ethnography was behind an attempt I made to visit Sukhumi's Institute of Gerontology, but then war broke out there and for all I knew the institute went the way of the Abkhazian library, torched by fleeing Georgians.

I asked the philosopher how he thought his grandfather had managed it, and he said: 'He never worried about anything in the whole of his life.'

But there was something else about that centenarian, about the trips his grandson said he had made down to Gori at harvest-time, his cart loaded with grain and fruit, and the cousin he had stayed with there, a shoemaker, whose son was 'the devil of a boy' who required frequent clips around the head to stay in order. The shoemaker's son was called 'Soso', an abbreviation of the Ossete 'Suslan', or of Jozef. Either way, this philosopher beside me was the cousin of Soso Dzhughashvili, boy hooligan, son of an Ossetian artisan and in later years known under a number of aliases as Ryaboi ('Pockmark'), Melikyants, Nishar-adze, and by others as the Butcher of the Kremlin, Uncle Joe, and Stalin.

The road to South Ossetia was not really a road at all. It ran unmetalled between rain-quarried cliffs. It made the bus dance to the rhythm of its potholes. At one point it simply disappeared beneath a recent deposit of rock, and for a moment the debating stopped, the scholars gripped their seats and the bus went over the edge, down a slope of alder, along a stretch of sand and into the river. There its wheels bounced and half-floated across a bed of egg-round boulders. No one spoke again until the wheels had locked into the far bank.

'The rain,' observed a historian, 'has run away with the road.'

But for the South Ossetians, this road was a lifeline, the only real link to the outside world. The war with the Georgians had reached a stalemate. The fighting was over and, in the manner of recent conflicts, minorities had fled to territory where they could be majorities – Georgians to Georgia, Ossetians to Ossetia. Finding themselves surrounded on three sides by hostile Geor-gians, and on the fourth by ten-thousand-foot mountains, the South Ossetians did the only thing they could. They drilled a hole through the Caucasus.

At the tunnel, the Russian border guards were sleepy. They did not have much to do. They mistook me for an Ossetian delegate and waved us all through. It was fine and sunny on the Russian side but beyond the tunnel in South Ossetia we came out into thick cloud. A group of Ossetian irregulars flagged down the bus and joined it. Their fatigues were soggy with rain. Water ran from the barrels of their guns and dripped onto the academics. South Ossetia was a grim, war-beaten place. Yet I could not suppress a smile, an overriding sense of relief. I had left Russia.

Not far beyond the tunnel, an archaeologist dipped into his bag and pulled out a semi-glazed earthenware vessel. It was an Alan lamp, he said. He'd found it here the previous summer with Pushkin.

'Pushkin?'

'He is the doctor here. A great man! You should talk to him.'

'How do I find him?'

'Just ask anyone.'

At the next village, I left the bus.

Pushkin! When I think now of these high Ossetian valleys, it is your voice I hear ringing out around the bare peaks, your rage and laughter. I see your tangle of grey hair and your blue eyes, the slow and steady pace you kept on the mountain paths. I think of your family and the animals and the iron bedstead on the balcony where you slept, where you still sleep, from the last frost of one winter until beyond the first of the next, where each morning you rise, shake the dust from your hair and offer a roar to the mountains.

Your house had a red cross daubed on the door and you would shoo out the hens when your patients came, sit them down in the wood-store and treat them with whatever remained of your medical supplies. That was your hardest battle, you said: you needed to be a mafia king to get the drugs nowadays.

I think of that first afternoon in the cookhouse with the

chicks hopping over the threshold and pecking at the floor, and the magazine picture of Brezhnev on the wall and the rain fizzing on the stove-pipe outside. We were waiting for the weather to clear in order to reach the far villages. I was impatient and rose to look through the window.

'Sit down,' you growled. 'The rain started at midnight, and it will stop at midnight.'

Natalya was kneading dough by the stove and your son and daughters with the balalaika were singing a eulogy to the vanished kolkhoz.

What a kolkhoz it was! The finest in the union! Four hundred cows, four thousand sheep! Yaks with their coats to the ground! In October the sheep would leave, up the valley towards the pass, and you all turned out to watch them go. From other kolkhozes in other valleys the flocks came and merged until, you said, there were fifty-seven thousand of them crossing the pass and flowing down to the Terek, through villages of Ingush, of Chechens, of Russians and Lamaist Kalmyks, until they reached the boggy pastures beside the Caspian Sea. For five and a half months up here you waited. You waited while the snow built up at the door and the rivulets turned to ice, you waited while the stones froze together and the ravens flew down and pecked in the yard. You waited for the day when the valley was again flooded with that vast white tide of sheep.

Natalya raised one floury hand and twisted it. 'They just opened it up and sold everything. The kolkhoz is good now only for birds to nest in.'

And you, Pushkin, the cat on your knee, your face stormy with anger, the traces of your hair refusing to lie flat. You could never disguise your fury at what had passed, at the stolen flocks and the fighting, at the wounds treated with dressings you tore from the shirts of your children, the week-long line of refugees fleeing up to the tunnel. But nor would you let it stay. You would shrug off your temper like a dog shaking water from its coat. And your laughter was just as sudden. It burst out in giggles that you seemed unable to control. It was the laughter of those who spend their lives in remote places, who swell with the immensity around them until they can contain it no more.

You turned to me and said, while the rain beat at the mud outside: 'I cannot think of a good reason why we should not have a drink.'

And that is the other memory of those mountain days, the scooped-out cow-horn with its foul-tasting *arak*, and even now, Pushkin, it makes me wince to think about it.

Pushkin was right. The rain stopped at midnight. We would set off for the villages in the morning. At dawn, wearing a bright orange shirt, he went to visit a woman who was ill. I crossed the valley, climbed the opposite slope and sat at the foot of a ruined tower.

To one side the river cut deeply into the hillside. Pennants of mist flew from the peaks. Above them the sky was blue. The sun was not yet above the mountains but its rays already fanned out from the ridge and there was the burning place where it would appear.

It reached the tops first, silvering their rocky finials. It slid down the high gullies and down the snow patches and down the upper slopes which looked bony and old without trees, and its light fell on the groups of pine below and on the outcrops and on a herd of brindled cows and the ruins of the abandoned houses and soon it had filled the whole valley.

The sound of the river rose from the ravine. A fragile warmth crept in with the sun. And far up the valley, an orange dot came out of one of the homes, let out a faint farewell roar and started its descent towards me.

*　　*　　*

'There'll be a lorry or something.'

Pushkin was confident of a lift, but we'd met no one all morning until a shepherd appeared on the road.

'Aleksandr Sergeyevich,' he said breathlessly, 'the bridge is in the water.'

Which explained two things – why we'd seen no vehicle, and why Pushkin was called Pushkin; he shared the poet's first name and his patronymic.

Pushkin was the only doctor and he tried to visit the high villages at least once a fortnight. He took with him no medical supplies – nothing at all in fact, not even a bag. Sometimes on the path he would bend down and pick a flower or a seed-head and say: 'This one I use for the stomach ... you put this over an infected wound ...'

At one place he pointed high above us, to a tottering homestead, and we climbed up to see a man whose face was shrivelled and blank with pain. He clutched his side and looked up at Pushkin. There was nothing anyone could do. Pushkin moved about the darkened room with a studied assurance, offering little more than his presence and the priestly boom of his voice: drink this tea, avoid the cold. He tickled the ear of the man's dog, asked about his daughter, and with a cheery pat on the shoulder, left him. Outside again in the sun, Pushkin said: 'Next time I come, he'll be dead.'

We walked much of that day. At first the track followed the course of the river, then struck up through the forest to a high ridge. From the ridge we looked back and saw below the shining roofs of the village, the threads of the river, and to the west a skyline of snow-topped peaks.

Pushkin was a tireless walker, not fast, but one who walked without really being aware he was walking. On occasions he would sink himself into some deep private contemplation and I watched his forehead as it wrinkled and the little black bulls of his eyebrows edged towards each other. His head would drop further, the black bulls would twitch – and then all at once he would shake his head violently, straighten up and cry: 'How are the legs? Normal?'

'Normal.'

'Watch the altitude.'

The altitude was one of Pushkin's favourite diagnoses. It was given as a blanket explanation for the failings of anyone who did not come from the mountains. If I was tired, it was the altitude. If I was slow at understanding something – altitude. When in the evenings, in some ill-lit house, he had set us both off on a bout of helpless laughter, he would look at me and splutter: 'Don't worry, it's just . . . altitude.'

On the second day, not far from the village of Edica, we heard shooting. The leaves parted and a man appeared on the road ahead with a Kalashnikov. Pushkin stopped, then let out a roar.

'Batraz!'

They embraced. The man wore a black shirt and had a teaky, sunburnt complexion. He'd been hunting. He was very keen on his gun and from time to time as we walked would loose off a few rounds at nothing and then turn and grin. In the end he ran back into the trees and for a long time afterwards we could hear the intermittent chatter of his shooting.

Pushkin flinched each time he heard it. 'What use is all this shooting?' He muttered for some moments and his pace quickened. Then he began a story, and with the telling of the story he relaxed.

It was the winter of 1973. Two metres of snow had fallen in the upper valleys. One night down in Roka he'd heard, above the hiss of the wind, a thumping. He leapt out of bed, threw open the door and there was a shepherd up to his waist in snow. (Pushkin's stories were always told with great drama.)

'It's a woman in Ermani, Pushkin,' the shepherd gasped. 'She can't have her baby!'

It took most of the night to reach the village. When they arrived, there were hundreds of people at the house. Pushkin turned to them and said: 'Get out! Everyone get out!' Then he looked at the woman. 'What did you call me up here for? This woman's dead!' But then she moved and he seized her wrist and found a slight pulse. So he shouted again: 'All of you get out!' The woman's great-grandfather – he was 135 – came up and said: 'Do anything, Pushkin. I would give my life to see her live.' Well, Pushkin just shoved him out with his boot. He set to work and both the mother and the child survived.

'And that was the child? With the gun?' I asked.

'That was him.'

We carried on for a while and Pushkin's frown deepened and the black bulls tiptoed together. 'But if it happened now, I would not have the things to save them.'

The following day we reached a village where one muddy path wound between a cluster of houses. Pushkin knew a family there who lived in a two-storeyed house – livestock below, three rooms above. Sons and granddaughters sat around the table, and all evening the grandmother lay on a bed in the shadows, staring at the ceiling. On the wall was a montage of five faces.

'Aunts and uncles,' they explained. 'This one 120, she 115, she 123 . . .'

'And your grandmother?'

'She is only ninety-five.'

In the morning, one of the women said: 'I will show you the gravestone.' She led us out of the village to a small knoll. The stone was spangled with lichen and was well weathered. 'This,' she said, 'my eldest uncle and aunt.' The wind was swinging

the hair across her face. On the side of the stone was written:
'. . . 165 years . . . her husband . . . died 173'.

As we left the village, I asked Pushkin: 'Do you believe these
numbers?'

'Of course. It was how old they were.'

'But why are there none now?'

'We eat yeast.'

'Is that all?'

'Everything's different now.'

To Pushkin, these elongated lives were just one of the
vanished riches of the Soviet past, like a full medicine cabinet,
like the kolkhoz sheep, like peace between the peoples of the
union.

But claims of longevity are not confined to the Caucasus.
Cicero's wife died at 103. In 1635, at the alleged age of 154,
Thomas Parr was presented to Charles I of England; he'd had
a child in his 120s, and the child himself lived to the age of 123.
Also 154 was a woman in Moscow who in the 1950s could still
recall meeting both Pushkin and Nekrasov. In 1958, a veteran
of Colombia's war of independence died in Bogotá at the age
of 169.

The Andes in southern Ecuador are known for their long-
lived people, as are the Hunza uplands of Kashmir. But nowhere,
it seems, is more conducive to long life than the Caucasus and
Transcaucasus. Soviet statisticians worked out that in the union
as a whole the number of centenarians per hundred thousand
people was eight; in Armenia it rose to twenty-five, in Georgia
thirty-eight, in Azerbaijan as a whole forty-nine – while in the
enclave of Karabakh there were as many as sixty-nine.

Soviet scientists showed a keen interest in longevity, believing
that long life, like everything else, was just a question of the
right policies. Symposia of gerontologists were convened and
whole institutes dedicated to its study. In 1967, on the fiftieth

anniversary of the October Revolution, Brezhnev was able to boast that Soviet citizens were now able to look forward to an average lifespan of seventy years. In the past, under the tsar, Russia had had Europe's lowest life expectancy – thirty-two years was all a Russian man could expect in 1897. Since the end of the Soviet Union, the figure has fallen again to fifty-seven and a half.

In Moscow I'd come across a book with the alarming title *May You Live to be 200!*, which included a sketch of the work of Professor Manuel Aliyevich Ibrahimov of Baku's Institute of Advanced Training of Physicians. He'd spent several years interviewing these long-livers and, while duly suspicious of pointing to any one cause, picked out certain common features of their way of life:

Diet. Typically 2500–3000 calories per day. Limited alcohol. Great amounts of tea, no coffee. Plenty of pomegranates, not much bread, a great deal of dairy produce and boiled, lean meat. Many walnuts. His old people tended to maintain their weight as it was at thirty.

Work. Routine important. Walk at least five kilometres a day and carry on working all your life.

Attitude. Avoid negative thoughts and excessive emotions. One man of 155 attributed his age to never having envied anyone in his life and to not seeing people who annoyed him. Adapt to change, be gregarious.

Sex. Continue regularly. Many centenarian men became fathers, ascribing their potency to a combination of honey and walnuts.

Pushkin said he remembered lots of old people. As a boy he knew a man who was already seventy when he'd become cook to General Yermolov, the Russian conqueror of the Caucasus. But the oldest person he remembered was a woman who at the age of 194 was still able to thread a needle. She died, he explained, not from disease but when she went to visit a friend and was swept off the path by an avalanche. And if it wasn't for the avalanche – who knows? – she might still be alive today.

It was dusk when Pushkin stopped suddenly in his tracks, and ducked down. Up ahead, smoke was seeping from a fire. We remained there for some time, then crept out in a large arc and rejoined the path a little way up.

'Chechens,' he whispered.

We carried on in the darkness to Ermani. Fireflies spun and glowed in the still air; Pushkin was nervous, and at the slightest noise we stopped.

The village of Ermani was the highest of them all. Pushkin claimed it was the highest village in the old union. Beyond it was just the mountains, and the frayed edge of the self-proclaimed Ossetian republic. It was up here that the Alan lamp had been found. We stayed with a family in a house with one big room and beds running top to toe all around the walls. They knew nothing about any Alan lamps. Just the horn, they said. That's what the Alans invented – the horn for drinking. You put it down on the table, like this, and it just won't stand up, so you have to drink. The Alans invented that.

There were three sons and they looked after the sheep that remained when the kolkhoz had gone. The village had been abandoned once, but in the fifties people were always coming here to settle. Under Brezhnev it had been wealthy. We all sat around the table and the paraffin lamp threw a dim light onto their hardened faces.

The mother pulled a cushion of bread from the oven. 'We're not waiting for a better life now. We just ask for our health.' Her sons flicked through magazines and talked about the times of the kolkhoz. The magazines showed pictures of combine harvesters in fields of honey-coloured wheat. They were dated April 1967, October 1963 and July 1965.

The early sun was warm on the flagstone step. It was another breathtaking Caucasian morning. Above the village, bright snow shone in patches near the mountaintops. Tiny, cream-coloured clouds drifted over the valley. From the peaks the cliffs dropped to slopes that greened and softened and opened out into pasture that was so full of flowers it was in places hard to see the grass. Far up the valley, a column of smoke rose from the camp of the Ossetian border guards. The sun had just cleared the ridge.

Across the yard came Kolya, the flaxen-haired twelve-year-old grandson of the household. He had a stick which he dragged behind him in the mud.

'Uncle Philip!'

'Yes, Kolya.'

'Where is Lake Chitixaca?'

'In South America.'

'Is that near your home?'

'No.'

'Is Tokyo?'

'No.'

'Do you have snakes?'

'Some.'

'I killed a snake last week.'

'Really?'

'It was thicker than my leg!'

'How did you kill it, Kolya?'

'I drank a special Indian tea that was so strong that if it bit, it didn't matter.'

'Amazing!'

'Do you have elephants with you?'

'No.'

'Volcanoes?'

'No.'

'We have volcanoes. That mountain over there is a volcano and I slept there last night with my sheep.'

'How many sheep do you have?'

'Thirty-nine!'

'That's a lot of sheep.'

'Yes, and once I was a sportsman and I had a gun and shot at the sky and ran all over those mountains and jumped from that one and fought in the kolkhoz way. I have only three sheep actually but one died. When I'm older I want to be an executioner. Do you know Bruce Lee? He fights in the kolkhoz way –'

At that moment Kolya spotted a lamb that had strayed into the yard. He chased it out onto the dried-mud path, out beyond the stockades and into the unfenced pasture where the flocks grazed in the glare of the moutain sun.

A little later, I walked with Pushkin up to the snowline. By the ruins of a watchtower we came across the Ossetian border guards. They lived in two large camouflage tents. It was their job to try to stop the Georgians getting in, or the Chechens. Their commanding officer pointed to the ring of peaks and we could just see the position of his men on the skyline. He put a grenade-launcher on Pushkin's shoulder and showed him how to sight the target.

Pushkin snarled and handed back the weapon and began a story about how, armed with only a stick, he had seen off a group of Georgian commandos. The Georgians had landed in a helicopter. He had gone up to them and said: 'Get out, this instant!' And they just laughed at him, and then he said there were four snipers with their long-range rifles trained on them and if he raised his stick they would shoot at once and there would be nothing left of them but ashes. 'Well, those Georgians just jumped back in their helicopters as if the earth was on fire!'

That night, Pushkin was in fine form. It was late and the light from the paraffin lamp shone yellow on the faces of the Ermani family. Pushkin poured a horn of *arak*, raised it to heaven and said: 'I have a joke.'

He started chuckling at once. 'Some Americans came and they said – Let's see what these Caucasians are made of! So they went up to a man and said – Farmer, here is some two-hundred-degree spirit. Drink it. We want to see what happens.'

(Pushkin throws back his own drink.)

'Fffaaaah! So he drinks it and then goes back into his field of corn and he farts – and by God, he burns a hole right through his trousers!'

(Pushkin is finding it hard to stifle his laughter.)

'Then two men come into his field and say: Why are you – it's the Americans again, but he doesn't recognise them – Why are your trousers burned? And why is your finger stuck up your arse? And he says to them: That's because some rascals came by and gave me the devil's own spirit, and now I don't want to lose, I don't want to lose –'

(Pushkin is banging the table with the cow-horn.)

'– the whole crop!'

Pushkin doubles up. He repeats the punch-line whenever he is able to draw breath. And I am laughing too, laughing at Pushkin laughing, and he thinks it is the punch-line and repeats it and I am hoping to God he will stop. But there is no sign of it. I blame the altitude.

And here is Pushkin again the next day, in another village, with his hazel stick studding the mud as he strides down from the ridge and he is shouting 'Hoa! Hoa!' at every living thing he comes across – dogs, bullocks, pigs, children – lunging at them and yelping, and leaping up on a log to talk over the fence to a woman who has just had a child and who wonders, wonders if the rash he has developed will ever leave the poor boy – her little crumb! – in peace.

School No. 5

Pushkin told me about three Russians living at an old copper mine some distance down the valley. On the way to Chinvali, capital of South Ossetia's improvised republic, I called in on them.

A grassy track led up to the wheelhouse. Stacks of rust-red steel lay beside it. The weeds of the valley had started to reclaim the mine – the wheelhouse, the machinery, and the chipboard cabin where I found Valery and Andrei playing chess.

'What brings you to this holiday resort?' asked Valery.

I told him I'd been up the valley looking for old people. 'But they were all dead.'

'That is hardly surprising.'

I told him too that I was on my way to see the Doukhobors on the far side of Georgia.

'So we're not the only Russians stuck down here?'

Andrei leaned forward and tapped my arm. 'How about a hundred grams?'

The chess was cleared away and Andrei uncorked the vodka. With the light fading, Valery lit a couple of candles. Volodya, the third of them, came in and kicked off his boots.

'We're onto the second row already,' he announced, and placed a bowl of muddy potatoes on the table.

Six months had elapsed since this skeleton crew had been sent down here from Russia, sent down to keep the tunnels dry and wait for better times. No one had paid them for four of those months and now they did not even have the money to return home.

'The Ossetians are good to us,' said Valery. He was stripping the mine away, selling it to them piece by piece.

A bare bulb flared suddenly and the fridge shook and whirred into life. Valery blew out the candles. Andrei slid a record from its sleeve and the crooning of Vladimir Vysotsky filled the hut.

'Our bard,' he said. 'He is our Bob Dylan.'

'No Longer Evening', 'No Shelter' – Vysotsky waded through his songs as if at any moment he might sink beneath them. The three miners lapsed into silence, each directing his gaze at a different point in the shadowy cabin. They were of a certain generation, these stranded miners – the Brezhnev generation, the Vysotsky generation. By the time they came of age, the Soviet Union was already dead. Brezhnev was kept going with sedatives and sleeping pills. Vysotsky drank, and died of drink in 1980; Brezhnev survived for another two years, and now, in the new Russia, there was no place for those passive souls raised under their sign.

Outside it was dark; through the open door came a cold mountain breeze. Andrei grasped the bottle. 'I was thinking.'

Valery laughed. 'Here's trouble.'

'These old people of yours – I think I know why they lived so long.'

'Why's that?'

'It was habit.'

'Rubbish, Andrei!' Valery scoffed. 'How can you live out of habit?'

'No, listen. Most people live to about sixty or seventy. When they get to eighty or ninety, everyone starts to tell them they're old. Right?'

'Right.'

'Well, if everyone's telling them that, soon they start to believe it. And that's their mistake.'

'What's their mistake?'

'Thinking they're old. If they think they're old, they just die. But if they do happen to make it to a hundred, people give up saying it. They just get bored. So those old people go on living.'

Valeri shook his head.

'It's true, Valery.'

'It's shit.'

Volodya, the third one, sighed and took up the potatoes and went out across the yard to the canteen. When we joined him later, the smell of cooking filled the dining-room. He had laid the corner of one table. The other tables were covered with magazines, litter, old chess sets, machine tools, dust. Beside the hatch to the kitchen was a red felt board, marked 'MENU'. A piece of paper was pinned to it on which Volodya had just written the day's date, and:

> *Soup*
> *Fried Potatoes, Kolbasa, Cheese*
> *Tea or Coffee*

Volodya had put on a white apron to serve it. These three forgotten exiles in their mine – afflicted as they were with the patience of ages – had standards to keep up. Or maybe it was just habit.

In the morning I left the miners and continued south. The republic's only main road dropped down from the mountains towards the capital. Chinvali was a town besieged. The Georgian front lines were close enough for them to have fired a grenade right through the bronze chest of Lenin. He stood near the abandoned railway station, daylight filling the wound in his back. For want of any better alternative the administration had left him standing and remained wedded to his discredited *apparat.*

Only one hotel was in operation in Chinvali and only one room was available – the Party suite, a bizarre series of four rooms: bedroom, bathroom, kitchen and a sitting-room with three sofas. A long table ran down the middle of the sitting-room. There was no electricity and no water.

That night, hunting for food in the lampless streets, I headed for the glow of the town bakery. Three women bent over the underground oven alternately fuelling it with brushwood and slapping ovals of dough against its walls. A turtle-necked man stood there with me waiting for the next bake. He said: 'I don't have much at home, but come back anyway.'

It turned out he was the republic's deputy president. At his home was a journalist from Rostov, a Don Cossack. I told him I'd been there some months before and he smiled: 'We say Rostov is the mother of crime and Odessa is the father.'

The deputy president put a jug of wine on the table. 'Last time you were here, the war broke out. You remember?'

The journalist nodded.

'We had to race through the streets without headlights.'

'With the shells falling all around!'

'And you wrote an article calling me a murderer.'

'Did I?'

'I have kept it.'

The deputy president watched the journalist, enjoying his unease. It wasn't hard to believe that there was some truth in what he'd written.

The outbreak of civil war in 1991 brought out not only the usual baffling savagery, but also a series of strange sightings. A great many people saw the craft which appeared one morning in the skies over Chinvali – fifty metres long and matt black.

It had hovered above the town for several minutes in complete silence. Someone had already drawn it for me that day:

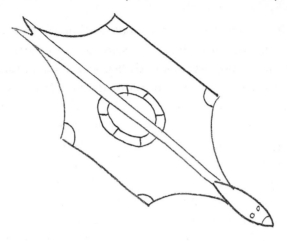

The deputy president said he had a video of it. But when I asked to see it, he gave an ambiguous smile, and reminded me that there was no electricity.

St George was also a frequent visitor at this time. In North Ossetia his gleaming mounted figure had appeared one winter's night in Digora. He'd urged a number of women to curb the drinking of their menfolk; there were difficult times ahead. One of the women said the saint asked her for a glass of milk. In the morning the whole town saw the tracks of his horse in the snow.

In Ossetia, as elsewhere, St George overlays a much older heroic cult. In these mountains his name is interchangeable with the home-grown saint, Uastardji. (Home-grown he might be, but his name bears a close resemblance to '*wasta*', the Arabic for 'intercessor' – in its secular sense – while '*–dji*' is a Turkish suffix.) It is to Uastardji that numerous roadside shrines are dedicated. For him Pushkin the doctor had reserved his finest performances: sacerdotal, booming, he would raise the cow-horn of *arak* to heaven and cry: 'Uas–tar–dji!' I could never quite tell if the drama was genuine.

The cult of St George and Uastardji is more important and certainly more prevalent than the Christianity the country professes to believe in. Every Ossetian festival begins with a toast to God and Uastardji; it ends with one to Uastardji alone. He is particularly potent for two weeks in November, and weddings conducted at this time are guaranteed to last. Enter an Ossetian house, and to the right of the door you will see a corner set aside for Uastardji, more often than not a picture of him on a winged horse. In the equine cultures of the Scythians, the Sarmatians and the Alans, a winged horse was a representation of the sun, while the moon was represented by the figure on its back.

In Georgia, the Tetri Giorgi – 'White George' – is the name not only of the lunar deity, but of a group of fervent Georgian nationalists. St George is the Georgians' patron saint, and in the thirteenth century the Latin Patriarch Jacques de Vitry wrote of their appearance in Jerusalem:

> These men are called Georgians, because they especially revere and worship St George, whom they make their standard-bearer in their fight with the infidels, and they honour him above all other saints.

That the Georgians so esteem St George is certainly true – but it is not the reason they are called Georgian. That is adapted from '*Gurj*', the name Arabs and Persians always used for this ancient Caucasian people.

In the Ossetian pantheon, the St George/Uastardji figure has only one serious rival, and that is the number three. Three is the mark of divine order, the primary bundle, and any worldly endeavour that imitates it is at once blessed. Ossetian women bake three pies as a prayer; men make three toasts (or three times three); newly-weds must walk three times around the hearth of their new home. Man is born, lives and dies; three generations make a century; mother, father and child constitute the perpetual equation of life. The smith, that pagan priest, wields three tools: anvil, hammer and pliers.

And so the list goes on. It does not take long in Ossetia to feel the creeping infection. You start noticing threes everywhere – three-legged stools, three spinning eagles above the cliff, three claps of thunder. Uastardji himself is not exempt from this obsessive threeism – the fine winged steed he rides has only three legs.

When the next morning I went to see the republic's president, I was not surprised to find him an expert on the cult of Uastardji (he'd done his masters degree on the subject), and that he was more willing to talk about 'the importance of Uastardji in times of crisis' than affairs of state. The austerity of his desk, from which stretched a runway of a conference table, was broken only by three telephones – yellow, grey and red. When the grey one rang, it was his secretary; when the yellow one rang, it was his wife. The red one remained silent. For all I knew, that was the one reserved for Uastardji himself.

The room was a shrine. Two steel-framed beds, white counter-panes, linoleum floor, a carpet on the unplastered wall. We sat there in silence, the three of us, the father on one side, one of the widows on the other. On the table between the beds was a starched cloth, a bottle of mandarin vodka, a fir-cone, and photographs of the two boys. They had been killed exactly three years earlier, and today was the day of their commemorative feast.

The younger one was hit by a sniper. He tumbled as he crossed the open ground beside the stadium. Two days later his brother died in a car crash. His widow, beside me, had also been in the car. For a month she lay in a coma, not knowing what had happened; then when she went to the grave of her brother-in-law, she was told: 'Your husband lies here too.'

We ate downstairs, ten of us in all. The door was open. I could see the sun in the yard outside and beyond it were the burnt-out houses and beyond them was a low hill and that was Georgia.

The boys' father stood and spoke. Tears formed in his eyes. 'My father was a baker. When I was ten they took him to war and I never saw him again. War has taken my sons too, and now I know their shadow better than my own life.'

For the first time in three years he drank. He sat down and remained damp-eyed and said nothing more. All around him was eating and talking and joking but he sat in silence until the meal ended and he rose. 'I must thank you all for being here today. I will ask you now to come with me to School No. 5.'

School No. 5 was in the west of the town, in an area of burnt-out cars and damaged buildings. At the entrance lay the rusting carapace of a bus. The school was no longer a school but a cemetery. They lost the old burial ground to the Georgians early on in the fighting, and somehow the idea took hold that the only place to bury those who fell was in the playground of the school that many of them had only just left. We stood at the boys' graves. Their father poured a glass of brandy, drank half and scattered the rest on the graves. To each of us in turn he handed the glass and we did the same.

He then ran a hand over the smooth summit of his head and looked out towards the plains. 'I cannot say now that if I heard someone speaking the Georgian language I would not kill them for the death of my two sons.'

In the end it was not a problem crossing the front lines. You had to walk across one set of lines into a tiny enclave of Georgians, then take a bus that recrossed the lines, dashed through Ossetian territory and stopped only beyond the main check-point, in Georgia proper. The number of destroyed buildings increased at the lines. The Russian peacekeepers dozed on their tanks.

The bus then sliced between maize-yellow fields to the plains town of Gori and its press of heavy, unfamiliar heat.

In the centre of Gori is a museum complex – two classical buildings and a railway carriage. One of the buildings is built over the top of an old brown hut. It was in this hut that Stalin was born, in which he was raised. It was in the railway carriage that he travelled. In an upper room in the third building stands his death-mask. Being used to the more usual, swollen iconography the only thing that struck me about Stalin's life-size death-mask was how very small it looked.

A woman shooed me out of the museum but I needed no shooing. It was already late afternoon and I was keen to reach Tbilisi before dark.

Rabbit Samvel and the Yezidi

The bus was three hours late. Tbilisi would be dark when I arrived, and at this time Tbilisi was not the sort of place to wander around at night.

'They will shoot you in the road.'

Samvel made a gun from his outstretched arm. He was half-Armenian and half-Georgian and a little more than half-drunk, swaying in the aisle and talking loudly. 'Come, stay at my house. I'll kill my rabbit.'

'I'll stay, but you can spare the rabbit.'

'I shall kill the rabbit! We'll make *shashlik*.'

'No, Samvel.'

Samvel frowned. Behind him, the late sun was bright on the fields of the Kura valley. In the distance was the blue rise of the Caucasus.

'OK, my friend. Rabbit shall run about. I will kill another. I have lots of rabbits. You can take one to England.'

'He will need a visa.'

'I'll get him one!'

'He has a Georgian passport?'

'No. Soviet rabbit.'

'In that case they'll say he's a spy.'

'So we must kill him and make *shashlik*! What do you say?'

Samvel steadied himself against the seat. His face shone with excitement. He reached for his coat and pulled out of it a letter

216

from his girlfriend. He had received it that morning and it said he must come immediately to Tbilisi. She could not live without him. He must tell her exactly what he felt towards her, tell her frankly and exactly. She could not be sure of what might happen if he did not come at once and tell her frankly and exactly how he felt.

Samvel's family lived in Tbilisi's old town, in a couple of makeshift shacks on the edge of the Kura river. A dried-mud yard lay between the two shacks and in the middle of this space stood a squat little pomegranate tree, spreading its boughs over a wooden table. The table was on a slope and when Samvel's mother placed a jug there the cherry *kompot* sat at a strange angle to the jug's rim. Samvel's rabbits lived in a cage beside the table.

The hours of that evening slid past with the soupy swirlings of the Kura river. The moon rose above the hills, tangling in the twigs of the pomegranate. At midnight it broke free and started a slow arc across the open sky. And all through those hours we remained at the table, all of us moonlit and merry and Samvel's arm now wrapped around the neck of Tamara, and beside them his sister Jujuna and beyond her their mother too, and an aunt and an uncle all chattering in Armenian and Georgian and Russian, while from other yards and other homes spread the humdrum hum of Tbilisi's summer nights.

Through mud-brown alleys came the Yezidi. His step was light on car-tyre soles. His serpentine route took him turning and turning down paths that were dark and biblical with age. He ducked into the yard and the door banged closed behind him. From the billow of his shirt he pulled an *arak* bottle and placed it on the table. Jujuna looked up at him with affection.

'Drunkard,' she said.

'Not one drop has yet touched my throat.'

He took the bottle, poured three glasses and pushed them

around the table, saying: 'Sheikh – Pir – Murid. These are the castes of Yezidi.'

'And which are you?' I asked.

He raised the first glass. The moon shattered in its curves. 'Sheikh.'

'A Yezidi prince,' said Jujuna.

Samvel rose and plucked one of the rabbits from its cage. He held it up by the ears. Its back legs kicked in desperation. 'Mama – the knife!'

The Yezidi leaned forward and made a grab for the rabbit. He caught one of its legs. The rabbit fell on the table, wriggled free, then leapt to the ground and ran off across the yard. Samvel went after it, into the darkness.

Jujuna was talking about the trip she had made last month. Bulgaria she liked but Romania was full of Gypsies. She went to Istanbul and found a spangly leather belt in the bazaar – but down by the river, the dirt, my God, the dirt, and the smell and these filthy children. You have negroes in your country, she said to me, you understand how these dark ones smell. But the Czech republic, now there was a country. Clean and Western and no Gypsies.

'In Tbilisi we have always been very tolerant. When Brezhnev came, he made a speech of friendship.' Jujuna traced the figure 102 on the table. 'One hundred and two different peoples in Tbilisi, living in peace. That's how we lived in those days. Now listen –' In the distance, beyond the dog barks and baby cries, was the occasional sound of shooting. 'This filth. We need Stalin again to clean it all up.'

Samvel returned with the rabbit, went into the kitchen, and came out with a knife. The rabbit swung by its ears. 'Now, a proper meal for our guests!'

Jujuna rose and slapped Samvel. She took the rabbit and put it back in the cage. Samvel stood and looked at the knife and then went to sit by Tamara but she turned away from him. He sat on his own beside the rabbit cage then put his head on his hands. As he slept, the Yezidi told a story about a man falling from a mountain and Jujuna stared up at him with a credulous, loving stare.

And so it went on beneath the moon, that first evening in Tbilisi's timeless, centuries-smoothed old town while one by one and in silence, the perfect little buds of the pomegranate tree dropped onto the table. They fell on our heads and on our arms and on the sleeping head of Samvel. They fell in our glasses and on the rabbit cage; and from the trees on the banks of the Kura river they fell to spin in the grey waters and drift down to Rustavi and on towards the shores of the Caspian Sea where, it was said, the oil was so plentiful that as you walked you could not help it sticking to the soles of your shoes.

'I am easy to find,' said the Yezidi sheikh. 'I have an ice-cream barrow on the corner of Prospekt Tsereteli.'

But Tbilisi cast its spell upon me and pulled me into the labyrinth of its backstreets. In tottering wooden houses I wasted afternoons trying to find the brilliant polyglot Laz, the blind Assyrian who had visions of the apocalypse, the Crusader community, Gurdjieff's cousin, the Russian Priguny, or 'jumpers'. All of them turned out to be either phoney or non-existent. So I slowed down, forgot about them and settled into the city's natural sauntering pace.

In a room on the edge of the old town, on a stone-topped desk by the window, I made a neat stack of road-worn notebooks. Each morning I happily tinkered there and read, following the comings and goings and the standing-stills on the street below.

The landlady was a sleepy-eyed woman whose husband was a colonel in the Georgian special forces. He appeared after two days from a tricky operation flushing out a group of bandits to the south. And though I did not tell him he found out anyway that I had been in South Ossetia, and only an evening's frank and heavy drinking enabled me to remain under his roof. He then slept for two days and went back to the front.

Just across the street were the old city's baths. All that could be seen of them above ground were a few skin-coloured domes. Down the steps existed another world, a subterranean steam-filled world, where in cavernous rooms the bedrock yielded its hot sulphury waters. Running water being intermittent in the city at the time, I descended the steps twice a day. I soaked in the steam, poured the water over my head. In the café afterwards I drank tea from tulip glasses while the sun fell through pinpoint holes in the roof.

The café was run by an Armenian woman with a shrill and toothless laugh. 'They all come here. That one's Georgian; he's Azeri; he's Greek; he's Russian; he's Armenian. They're all friends when they come to drink my tea.'

Cigarette smoke drifted in the sun shafts. The buzz of conversation swelled and sometimes the door of the women's baths opened and the flap-flap of their shoes filled that steamy crypt.

I put him at about twenty but he may have been younger. He was sitting opposite me one morning telling me how he'd been caught near the baths when the fighting came in 1991. He'd run to hide in an upper room. He was very frightened. Four of them had come into the room to wait and when they'd changed their clips they broke open a medical pack and filled syringes from phials of morphine. 'It makes you less frightened,' they said. 'Have some.' He'd said no, and peered from the window as they left, as they ran crouching across the street and by the kiosk one of them fell and the boy was close enough to see the strange look of surprise on the man's face.

*   *   *

The Armenian church of Sourp Nishan had trees growing from its roof. An old woman was sitting outside it, in one of its blind arches. Her feet didn't quite reach the ground; beside her was an old leather valise. She was wearing a black scarf and a black dress and there were tears in her big blue eyes. She was called Mara and she had just arrived from Yerevan.

Don't worry yourself, she said, someone is on their way to help, someone she'd met and they were going to give her a room. She'd be all right once she had a room. It was just her head was in a muddle after the journey, but she'd be all right with a rest.

The Armenian priest in Tbilisi had told her it was up to her to arrange it. She had come up from Yerevan to bury her son. She hadn't seen him for a year or two now. They used to call him Apollo and he was tall as a statue. He was her only son; she had no one left now. He'd always been a good son but when he came here, he started to play with knives and no good comes if you play with knives. But don't worry yourself, she said, I will be all right once my friends arrive.

Several days later, I happened to see Mara again. She was in a metro station, stooping among the crowds with a fan of roubles in her hand. She was begging. Her two friends had come, she explained, the ones she'd met. They had a room for her and the man carried her case and the three of them walked off down the street. It was hot and they walked quite fast and Mara had to hurry to keep up. Soon there were people between her and her friends and she couldn't see so well. Then there were more people and crowds and a great square and she looked around and she couldn't see them at all.

Mara had gone then to find the documents of her son's flat. At the Housing Committee she was told to come back the next day, and the next day the same. After a week they said to her: the flat's been sold. So she went to the police and told them her flat had been stolen and what could they do about it? And they said, look, grandmother, go away and don't make trouble for us.

Now she could not bury her son and she had no money to get back to Yerevan and only the one black dress she stood in. When I gave her the money she said it was not that that worried her so much as having no spare dress. And when several weeks later I rang her in Yerevan to see if she'd got back, she said: yes, of course I returned safely, I had a good journey in the bus and met a lady from Spitak who'd lost her son in the war and we sang songs in her home in Spitak and do you know that she went to her cupboard and she had a whole row of black dresses – and she gave me two!

So please, Mara said, you're not to worry yourself.

One night that week there was a storm. I was visiting a man in the west of the city who had recently formed a 'Society of Pagan Philosophers'. This was the latest in a line of post-Soviet projects which began in 1991 when, with every cobbled-together group calling itself a nation, he had declared his apartment an independent republic. He had written a constitution, a bill of rights, set up a national park in the bathroom, and given interviews to journalists whose passports he had checked at the frontier, i.e. the front door. For all he knew the flat was still independent, but after the fighting in 1991 he'd lost interest in politics and let the republic to an American businessman.

We spent the evening drinking Georgian wine, and at midnight precisely a great blast of air shot down from the mountains, through the open window to slam closed a glass door with such force that it shattered. The pagan philosopher did not move from his armchair. He said it was the hand of the spirits without a doubt and his landlord deserved everything they sent him.

When I left the building a little later it had started to rain. The road was awash, little more than a running river. The water buffed my ankles. The noise was fearsome. Through the rain came the twin cones of a car's headlights. Inside, a man in a T-shirt sat hunched against the wheel. 'Get in!' he cried. Clearly the storm excited him, and it came as no surprise, as we were sluicing down a hill, that he lost control of the car, which spun through 180 degrees, bounced off the kerb and came to rest with its bows lodged in two feet of water. No amount of trying would start it again. I threw open the door, waded back to the road and flagged down the next car, which turned out to be a police car. The rain to them was a joke. That the windows didn't close was a joke too, and they laughed with more vigour the more wet they became.

Eight people died in the flood. The next morning the roads were covered in stones. In the sky drifted high and harmless clouds.

It was mid-afternoon. Tbilisi's crowds were dealing with the streets in their own way – the stork-thin women with bags raised to block out the sun, the peacock-flaunt of flowery-shirted men, the too-fat crooks with sunglasses, the swaggering sharks with pistols, the currency touts, the fruit-hawkers, the war wounded.

The Yezidi sheikh was there with his ice-cream barrow. He shut up shop and we walked through deltaic lanes to a high-sided courtyard – up an outside staircase, through screens of washing and then a room of bare boards, and three women in one corner of it.

When Pushkin came down to this region in 1829, he carried in his baggage a copy of Maurizio Garzoni's *Notice sur les Yezidis*. At this time Pushkin also made a point of meeting Yezidi troops on the Russian front. His account of it was, for me as well, the first encounter with this mysterious sect. The second was in Gurdjieff's *Meetings with Remarkable Men.* Gurdjieff remembered being told as a child that if you drew a circle in the dust around a Yezidi, it was impossible for them to escape. He himself had tried once to wrench a 'weak woman' from such a circle but found that he could not. If a Yezidi was to break out, he claimed, they would at once enter a state of catalepsy for a period of either thirteen or twenty-three hours.

I came across the Yezidis again during the Gulf War, in a town in the north-east of Syria. A teacher of English jabbed a finger towards two women sitting beside some springs: 'They are Yezidis. They believe in sitting.' I said I was sure they worked just as hard as anyone else, but what he'd actually said was that 'they believe in Satan' – and in doing so was peddling an age-old prejudice. Generations of European travellers had likewise tagged the Yezidis 'devil-worshippers', while among their closer neighbours they were known variously as 'light-extinguishers', 'dog-collars', 'hairy Kurds' and 'keepers of the eightfold beard'.

In truth, the Yezidis believe in Satan only in so far as the central figure of their belief is a fallen angel. But they call him Melek Taus, and will not utter the name Satan. Similar-sounding words are likewise forbidden, but when during persecutions Ottoman troops forced the Yezidis to denounce 'their God Satan', they did bring themselves to mumble 'Sultan' instead.

The Yezidis do not worship the devil. But they do accept in a way that distinguishes them from all the other faiths of this faith-soaked region that evil is an integral part of creation. Our universe is naturally flawed, they say, and to deny it is to miss an elemental truth. I could not help being drawn to this idea. It was a riposte to all those dreamers – from Christians to Communists – who clog their thinking with the way things should be and ignore the way they are, who gaze for too long at their own glittering visions and fail to see the glories in the twists and bumps that make up the real world.

The Yezidis claim descent from the seed of Adam, while ascribing to the rest of mankind (and all vermin) a common ancestor in Eve. They are a closed society and strictly endogamous, and although in their rites and beliefs there are traces of every belief in the neighbourhood – Zoroastrian, Christian, Manichaean, Judaic, Nestorian, Muslim, Sufi-Rafidi – theirs is a religion which contains elements which all these have lost.

The centre of the Yezidi faith is in northern Iraq, at the shrine of Lalish where rest the bones of their twelfth-century prophet. Born in the Bekaa valley, just as the Seljuk Turks swept into the region, Sheikh Adi studied in Baghdad under various Sufi teachers. He retired to a remote valley near Mosul, where his reputation for austerity spread. Each night he recited the entire Koran, twice. He lived off the fruit he grew and wore only his own home-spun cotton. By the end of his life, fasting had so wasted him that when he bent to pray, his disciples noted that his brains rattled in his skull 'like pebbles in a calabash'.

The ice-cream sheikh sat cross-legged and brooding. The sun slatted across the floorboards before him. He was not being forthcoming. The Yezidis were ethnically Kurds. I'd established that. (Although he later contradicted it.) He'd told me how each morning Yezidis were required to eat a little soil from the tomb of Sheikh Adi. He mentioned holy shirts but when I asked him, for instance, how Yezidi belief differed from the Zoroastrians, he would not be drawn.

'Really, I am not permitted to talk of these things. You must go to Armenia. There are more Yezidis there.' So on the way to finding the Doukhobors, I took a bus to Yerevan.

A high pass served as the Georgian–Armenian border. The wind blew down from the bare mountains. The border guards said nothing as they searched the bus. Beyond the border we pressed on between rock-littered slopes – the unchanging rock-littered slopes of Armenia – before starting the long descent to the Ararat valley.

Of Pearls and Peacocks

Aziz Tamoyan, political representative of Armenia's Yezidis, occupied a single back room of some larger concern. Outside the building two of his henchmen stood waiting, wide-shouldered men with pencil-thin moustaches. They toed out their cigarettes and in silence I followed them down a long, unlit passage towards a hairline of light. The door swung open into a room of dramatically small proportions. There were two desks. At one sat a woman before a typewriter, at the other was Tamoyan.

'Welcome,' he said, offering a power handshake (elbow against the ribs, forearm chopped down). He had a Levantine manner that was both proud and suspicious at the same time. His conversation did not err from the bloodless facts of a politician's speech. He read out extracts from his own newspaper – *The Voice of the Yezidis* – confirmed with census figures the position of the Yezidis as Armenia's largest minority, and was quick to point out how twenty-four of his people had recently died fighting 'the Turk' in Karabakh. And I nodded and took notes and asked questions that didn't interest me, and all the while I was distracted by the one thing in that room with any colour – the flag behind Tamoyan's shoulder: twin horizontals of red and white and a golden crest in the top left-hand corner, and inside it a peacock, surrounded by the spreading rays of the sun.

When Tamoyan left the room for a minute or two, I stood and crossed to the window. A screech like a wailing baby rose from the yard. Muscovy ducks swayed across a fenced-in polygon of grass. The screech had come from a peacock.

'It is yours?' I asked the typist.

'What?'

'The peacock. Is it a Yezidi peacock?'

She smiled. 'No. Not ours. It is another's.'

In 1911, Queen Mary discovered in a shop at the Kashmir Gate in Delhi the steel figure of a peacock. She was told by Mr Schwaiger the proprietor that it was 'the idol of the Yezidis of Mesopotamia'. The face half-hidden in its tail was said to be that of their prophet, Sheikh Adi. Mr Schwaiger assured the Empress of India that £2000 had recently been offered for the bird, but in honour of Her Majesty's visit he would like to present it to the British Museum. There it was put on display while Londoners queued up to examine this artefact of 'the Lucifer-Worshippers'. One of those to see the exhibit was a Yezidi expert who identified 'the impudent bird' as a trinket whose like was to be found all over Persia. Ten pounds would be a good price for it. The piece was quietly removed to the museum's vaults.

Peacocks briefly haunted the strange flights of George III. Practising a speech, he once decided that at the end of each sentence he should add the word 'peacock'. A good idea, suggested the attendant minister, but not the sort of word the people should hear uttered by their king. The silences, as the king mumbled 'peacock' to himself, gave the speech a rare gravitas.

Royalty and peacocks have frequently gone together. It was said that in ancient Persia when one king died a white peacock rose from his head and flew to another, thereby identifying the successor. And it was a white peacock that landed on the head

of the prophet Zoroaster. Other Indo-European mythologies –
Hindu and Greek – equate the bird and its tail with the sky.

But to the Yezidis the peacock is Melek Taus, fallen angel,
the Peacock Angel, who wept for seven thousand years and
extinguished the flames of Hell. Effigies of the Peacock Angel
were taken from village to village by the Yezidi *kocak*, a caste
of dancers who spun round the peacock in an ecstatic trance,
their long hair scattering pearls of sweat into the crowd. Sometimes it was not a peacock but a cock, and in this the Yezidis
share with the Scythians a representation of the first of all the
gods, the sun.

When Tamoyan returned, I asked him about the flag.

'The peacock, yes, he represents our god.'

'And the sun?'

'The sun is at the heart of it all. Which of us has seen Christ
or Moses, or Mohammed? Yet every morning when the sun
comes up we see the greatest miracle of all.'

Aziz Tamoyan told me of some Yezidis who lived in a village
called Zavouni.

On a warm morning, with the snowy dome of Mount Ararat
floating in the southern sky, I walked to the outskirts of Yerevan.
Volcanic rocks covered the slopes. Racks of pylons converged
on an electrical sub-station. A smudge of mud-walled houses
lay to one side and among these I came across a group of
women.

'Is this Zavouni?' I asked.

'It is Zavouni.'

'And are you Yezidis?'

'We're Kurds.'

They stared at me from half-bowed heads. The breeze ruffled
their skirts.

'We're not Kurds,' said another, 'we're Yezidi.'

'I'm a Kurd.'

'You're not. You're Yezidi.'

'We're just Kurds.'

'I am Yezidi and I will be a Yezidi until the day I die!'

It was this woman whom I asked where to find the community's leader.

The home of Pir Miras Namoy Khoudoyan was dark inside and earth-floored. His wife stood tossing a bobbin of wool, spinning it as it fell. His daughter paced the room, grinding a coffee-mill as though it were some awkward problem of the heart. Khoudoyan himself placed his elbows on the table and turned his tired gaze towards me. 'I am a pir. Pirs and sheikhs, we hold the spirit for the people. They believe we have powers.'

'And do you?'

'I don't know. But things happen.'

'Things?'

'A man had a dream that I'd hit him on the jaw. This was only last week. In the morning he had a terrible pain and he came to me and said: "Pir, my head's gone wrong in the night." So I took his chin in my hands and massaged it until it was better and the man gave me a sheep. That is the way it is with us.'

'I see.'

The pir's daughter laid coffee and fruit on the table. His wife said to him: 'What will you do with that?' She was pointing at a car engine that lay bleeding oil onto the mud.

'I will mend it later.'

He turned to me and started to talk of the hymns. In composing the prayers and hymns of the Yezidis, Sheikh Adi had always warned his followers against the written word. In this way he ensured the continuation of a fine oral tradition. But he also left the door wide open for regional discrepancy and the sort of poetic fermentation which is destroyed the moment a sacred text is written down (destroyed – and replaced at once by tedious textual squabbling). The Yezidi stories are kept by dynasties of pirs and sheikhs and it is in them that they have brewed and been flavoured by the centuries.

'Yes, it is true. We alone have the stories. It is not for ordinary people to know the stories. They can be heard but they cannot be told.'

'And are you permitted to tell me a story?'

He looked at me. His eyes were watery with age. 'If you wish I will tell you the first story.'

And he recounted his own version of the Yezidi creation myth. His gaze remained fixed upon me and a bare bulb glowed above his head:

'God created first a pearl and then a white dove. He put the pearl on the back of the dove and the bird and the pearl flew together for forty thousand years.

'Then God made Adam and placed him in Paradise and at the beginning he had no need to eat or drink. But Melek Taus the fallen angel came and gave him corn. Adam ate the corn and because he could not expel it he swelled and swelled and swelled [pir indicates this swelling with his hands]. Melek Taus then took Adam from Paradise. He placed him on a fruit tree and at that moment Adam acquired his physical shape and expelled the corn [pir makes defecating gestures]. The tree said to Melek Taus: "Why did you do such a thing, making me unclean?"

'And Melek Taus said to the tree: "Do not weep, tree. From your wood I will make a pillow, and there will be people who come and place their head upon you at night and in the morning will press their forehead against you in prayer and these people will be Muslims."

'Eve was created from near the armpit of Adam and together they had forty sons and forty daughters but when he saw how they argued, God sent them away and gave them all different languages to speak and that is how the world began.'

In another version, the pearl bursts open to release the angels and the waters of the sea; in yet another God kicks the pearl and thus are formed the mountains and the sky and all the flaws and imperfections of our flawed world.

I asked the pir about the pearl – the first thing, from which came all creation. And he said simply: 'The pearl was made from light.'

Light – always light. Light of the sun, light in the beginning, light as essence; light common to all faiths of this region, to Zoroastrians and Manichaeans, to the three monotheisms of the Book; light common to all the dogmatic believers I'd been with in the north – the golden light that came from the Molokans' statue of Maria the Spinster, the gilded light that sanctified the icons of the Old Believers, the shard of light in us all that had driven the Doukhobors on their centuries-long, iconoclastic odyssey.

The pir pressed his hands on the table and rose to his feet. From a wardrobe he took a suit. Sixteen medals paraded across it. In the Patriotic War he'd been a major and had received the Star of Stalingrad and had helped retake Minsk. One morning in Germany, he and an American officer arrived from opposite directions as the advance guards in a certain town. The American was a colonel from New Orleans. They saluted each other beneath the clock tower and I tried to picture these two displaced southerners, united in victory, standing together in a German town square.

He'd worn the suit when he went to Moscow. It was 1989 and with the war in Karabakh intensifying, the Armenians were emptying the Azeri villages in Armenia. They came to the Yezidis and said: 'You're Muslims too. You must leave.'

'We're not Muslim,' said the Yezidis. 'We're Yezidi.'

The pir was asked by the villagers to do what he could. He thought for a while and then decided to take the case to the top. As a veteran, he was able to see Gorbachev. He stepped into the office, his chest clanking with medals, and showed the chairman his passport. 'Here, it says Yezidi. We are not Muslims.' Gorbachev promised to lean on the Armenians and the Yezidis stayed.

'So you liked Gorbachev?'

He shook his head. 'Gorbachev was a fox.'

Pir Miras had been born in a village on the northern slope of Aragets. At the age of seven he had gone into the hills for his first summer with the sheep. He slept beneath the stars and learned to work the dogs and to pray – once before sunrise, once just after sunrise, at midday and at dusk. He had lived like that until the war and then after the war when he came home the villagers would not allow him to live in the village and he came to Zavouni.

Like all small, tightly-defined groups, Armenia's Yezidis had splintered into factions; they argued over rites and ethnicity and they argued over attitudes to Kurdish separatism but beneath all the high-sounding debates was just plain clannism. It is blood and not belief which really produces such passions.

When I asked Pir Miras if he would ever return to his village, he said simply: 'They would kill me.'

A low-level fog hung over the Araxes valley. The sun was bright above it, but at ground level there wasn't much to see. The doctor who'd driven me up from Yerevan said: 'Shamiram, it is somewhere here.'

His car left behind it a muffled silence. From the main road, a smaller road ran straight out across the plains towards the Turkish border and the Yezidi village of Shamiram.

The dogs began to bark before I reached the village. In the mist its metal roofs shone like haloes. Cockerels clawed at midden-tops. In the centre of the village stood a brand new monument. Monolithic, constructed of two-tone tufa, it was carved on all four sides. On one, a globe was balanced on a pair of outstretched hands. On another, facing south, was a representation of the shrine at Lalish in northern Iraq. On another was the figure of a man with a lance standing at the top of some steps.

A group of men had gathered: 'Do you know who it is?'
'Sheikh Adi?'
There was the sound of laughter.
Someone shouted: 'It is Melek Taus!'
'It is not!'
'It's our god!'
'It's not our god. He is invisible.'
'It is Zoroaster.'
Then one man stepped out from behind the group. He wore a black suit. He said to me: 'Leave, please. There's nothing for you to see here.'

I asked about the sheikhs and pirs, but they were in Moscow, in Yerevan, ill. The man repeated his order and I bowed, a little theatrically, and walked back to the main road.

Back in Yerevan I had more luck. I met an Iranian scholar who knew something of the Yezidis, and he said: 'You should see the Sheikh of Sheikhs.'

Go to Abovian, he told me, and ask in the meat market on the edge of the city. The Yezidis control the meat market.

Abovian is one of Armenia's larger cities. At the meat market were bristly men chewing sunflower seeds who looked through me when I mentioned the Sheikh of Sheikhs.

'People come from Syria to see Sheikh of Sheikhs.'

'. . . and Egypt also.'

'I too have come a long way.'

A man approached us, shouldering a side of mutton. I stood aside to let him pass. There was a little more seed-chewing, some seed-spitting, and then one of the men nodded up the road.

'You will find Sheikh of Sheikhs in house number six of the second street.'

Behind a large metal gate was a yard shaded by a walnut tree. A man stood beside the tree. 'Sheikh of Sheikhs,' he said, 'he is at a meeting. In two hours he will come. Or maybe four.'

Aslan was his son and one day he too would be the Sheikh of Sheikhs. He was squat and swarthy, with a boxer's hands. His own son was in the hills with the sheep but beneath the tree, surrounded by sisters and aunts, trussed and swaddled in blankets, was Aslan's grandson, youngest of the heirs to the sheikhdom, whom they called 'Two-Kilos' on account of his unusually low birth-weight.

Aslan showed me the large room which acted as the community's shrine. On one wall, above a vase of plastic dahlias hung a picture of Lalish. The other wall was a long cupboard covered by a faded velveteen shroud. 'This is what we pray against.' He touched his forehead to the cloth.

'And what is inside?'

He pulled back the shroud. Behind it was a vast hoard of blankets and mattresses and pillows. 'Guests,' he said by way of explanation, 'come from God.'

On top of this sacred linen-cupboard was a lace-bound reliquary. 'This you must not touch. It is our holy of holies.'

A year or two ago a policeman had come to search the house. Seeing the reliquary, he asked: 'What is inside it?'

'None but Sheikh of Sheikhs knows what is inside.'

But the policeman reached out for the reliquary, and as he did so, he felt his arm paralyse. He stood there in panic, unable to move, unable even to speak. He had to wait until the Sheikh of Sheikhs arrived to have the spell lifted.

The policeman had been searching for weapons; the day before there'd been an accident. Aslan's children had been playing with a gun and it had 'come alive'. Aslan pointed to a picture on the wall. 'She was my only daughter.'

The Sheikh of Sheikhs came in the late afternoon. We were sitting beneath the tree – Aslan, the women, Two-Kilos and me. One of the women had a packet of biscuits down her front, and from time to time plucked one out and offered it around. The gate opened and three men walked in. The Sheikh of Sheikhs was unmistakable in the middle, kingly in a high Astrakhan hat.

He shook my hand, gestured to his family to sit down and took a seat beside his son. They discussed the meeting he'd been to, some family matters and then quietly, and without prompting, the Sheikh of Sheikhs began to speak of the things that made up his faith – the transmigration of souls, the brothers of the hereafter, the spring festivals and winter fasts, the pearl, Lalish. And as he spoke, he kept his eyes fixed upon me. His face was a mishmash of sun-lines and crow's-feet.

'What is your interest in us?'

I told him that I'd heard the Yezidi belief was one of the oldest of all.

'It's true. All the other religions, they changed at one time or another. The people became Zoroastrian or Christian or Muslim. But the Yezidis, we have never changed.'

In the beginning, around the turn of the second millennium BC, the forebears of the Indo-Europeans are believed to have pushed south out of the Eurasian steppe. Six hundred years

later a great threat – probably repeated incursions by neighbouring tribes – coincided with the visions of the prophet Zoroaster.
He spoke of a world divided between good and evil, between
light and darkness, a world which is moving towards the
moment when it will all end and the souls of the dead will rise
again for judgement. This view differs fundamentally from the
one suggested by Yezidi cosmology – it is more combative, and
it is consummate.

The creation myths show the greatest divergence. Both the
Yezidis and the Zoroastrians agree that the world was created
from a pure proto-natural state (the pearl of the Yezidis, the
light of the Zoroastrians). But while to the Yezidis the transition
to the current world was made by a heroic act (the killing of a
bull, as in the cult of Mithra), the Zoroastrians hold that it is
the result of a war – a confrontation between the forces of
darkness and light, Satan and God. So, to the Yezidis the act
of creation was good, releasing light from its confinement; to
the Zoroastrians, it merely signalled the beginning of an unstable
era. The Yezidis in their more benign world see all time as
ever-present; Zoroaster taught that it would eventually be
redeemed.

Philip Kreyenbroek, in his study of the Yezidis, suggests that
the taboo on the word 'Satan' – which for so long earned the
Yezidis their 'devil-worshipper' tag – stems from the threat
posed by the newer Zoroastrian faith. The Yezidis banned the
word not because it was sacred to them, but because it was
what most clearly distinguished the newer belief from their
own.

In the Zoroastrian vision, the forces of good will eventually
triumph over evil; the allies of darkness will be cast into a sea
of liquid metal while the just ones emerge into warm milk.
As the first of the eschatological texts, the Zoroastrian Avesta
anticipates not only the Books of Daniel and Revelations, but

all those groups which promise an end to the corrupt ways of the world – the Old Believers and their Fourth Rome, the Molokans, and the Bolsheviks. With Lenin, scion too of steppe people, the vision of Zoroaster came full circle.

The Yezidi texts on the other hand suggest a world that is reconciled to its opposites. There is no struggle between good and evil, no attempt to rid the world of darkness. The Yezidis, it would appear, do not dream of warm milk, nor nurture a dread of liquid metal. They aim simply to avoid evil, rather than purge it. And in this they sidestep one of the great paradoxes of our earthly existence. For as any dictator learns, it is precisely what you try to purge that becomes your downfall. If you try to create heaven on earth, likely as not you end up with hell.

The sun was getting lower. It seeped through the leaves of the walnut tree, falling at random on the table and the dishes of fruit, on the women and Aslan, on the swaddled shape of Two-Kilos and on the face of the Sheikh of Sheikhs.

I asked him how his family came to be here and he told a blood-stained story which ended with guns and his dead granddaughter, and began with guns and his grandfather in a dusty village near Kars. His family had lived there for centuries. In 1915 the Turks set every community against itself, against the *giaours*, the non-Muslims in their midst – Armenians, Assyrians, Greeks and Yezidis. The Sheikh of Sheikhs (grandfather of the current one) felled a handful of Turks with his rifle as they came up the slope towards the village. But his ammunition was soon exhausted. The attackers took aim and shot him, but he did not flinch; their bullets would not touch him. They took rocks to him and they broke his bones. But the Sheikh of Sheikhs would not die, and so they dragged him off and burned him, and although in the flames his soul finally left him for another, his body remained intact and his assailants saw it and fled in terror. The family of the Sheikh of Sheikhs were able to recover the body and bury it before they themselves ran for the safety of the Russian lines.

Seventeen years later, under a different regime, the villagers again turned on their own neighbours. They pointed to the dead man's son, the new Sheikh of Sheikhs, and said: 'He is an enemy' – not *giaour* this time, but kulak. They took the Sheikh of Sheikhs and his heir to a jail in Yerevan. There the two Yezidi sheikhs were executed.

'I was too young at the time,' said the Sheikh. 'I was jailed later.'

'What for?'

'Murder.'

On coming of age, the Sheikh of Sheikhs had waited one night outside a certain house. When the owner returned he shot him. In this way he avenged the deaths of his father and brother. 'I killed only one, the rest of the guilty ones walked free. I was already the father of six children. Yet still I killed.'

I left the Sheikh of Sheikhs and headed north. Two days later, beneath the cone-shaped mountain of Aragets, I reached another group of Yezidi villages. On the mountain's slopes were their summer pastures. The land was bare, treeless. Warm Asiatic winds were blowing unchecked across its grassy tracts, flicking the neck-fur of the dogs, scooping up dust from the earthquake ruins.

They had been keening for days. The sound of it flooded from the window of the old kolkhoz office. Inside, an ellipse of women – scarved, hard-faced women – were seated around the body of a teacher. Daughters and sisters sat at his head. His widow rocked back and forth among them. The wailing around her rose and fell. She leaned forward and ran her hand through his hair, across his ash-grey face, and all at once she cried out and beat her temples and lunged at the body with such violence that the women were forced to restrain her.

An old man entered the room. His stick tap-tapped on the linoleum floor. With fabulous gusto he sang a lament for the man's life, recalling his proud and handsome face, his kindness as a father, his brilliance as a teacher, his faith as a man. The body lay still. Tumbling through the scales the old man's voice grew larger until it was too large for the room, and it spilled from the window and out into the eternal sweep of those high plains.

I walked out of that village and on to the next. The outstretched limbs of the mountain shadowed the houses. Half a wall of a fifth-century Armenian church stood as windbreak to a group of smokers. Two barefoot children were with them, chewing onions.

The sheikh of this village I found in his stove-room. A shaft of light pierced the centre of the roof. The beams were blackened by generations of smoke. They were stamped with the pale hoof-marks of Khouda Navi, the Yezidis' St George-like mounted deity.

'We make them each year with flour. He brings us luck.' The sheikh was an old man with droopy eyes. We sat opposite each other on car seats.

'The simple people think of these saints as real.'

'And do you?'

His fingers worked mechanically at a set of prayer beads. 'Saints are saints. But nowadays I find it difficult to know what's holy.'

It was getting late. For some time I continued north, following the main road. The mountains were tinged with wine-yellow light. The shadows rose up the slopes and with the dusk a truck passed, pulled to a halt and offered me a lift to the town of Gyumri. I hauled myself up into the cab, and there was the familiar smell of poor fuel.

'What is in the truck?' I asked.

'Stones.'

In this scarred, landlocked country, what else was there to transport but stones?

Tolstoy's Grave

In Gyumri, the truck driver introduced me to his cousin, a painter with the good Armenian name of Ararat.

Ararat lived in a house he'd just finished building with his own hands. Four children, his wife and his parents shared it with him. We stayed up late, talking outside beneath his year-old vines. The night was hot and heavy with insects and the sound of barking dogs and far-off arguments. Ararat remembered the day some years before when he had gone up onto the roof of his studio and lay there, quite flat, while beneath him the entire building quivered and shook.

'The noise,' he said. 'I can never forget that noise. It was like waves against the shore, but one hundred times stronger.'

When he had stood and walked to the parapet the landscape of his city had been transformed utterly. Twenty-six thousand people were dead. Now for him time was divided between before the earthquake and after the earthquake.

I slept on Ararat's sofa and in the morning asked him if he knew the Doukhobors. He said, yes, sometimes they came across the border to sell their cheese. In the market they told me they hadn't seen the Russians for a while, and it took some time to find a taxi driver willing to take me across the frontier, back into Georgia.

*　　*　　*

The village of Goryelovka is distinctive for its turf roofs, the storks on its abandoned chimneys, and the pale yellow hair of its children.

It had been many months since the Doukhobor in Moscow had pointed at the map and announced that it was here he'd been born, here 'on the edge of the world'. And now I was standing beside another Doukhobor, with a chin stubbled like a cactus and he was pointing to the windy place above the village, saying: 'The borders of three countries meet on that ridge, and not one of them's ours.'

They arrived here in 1841, driven south by a regime that valued nothing so highly as military service. They were Doukhobors, 'spirit-wrestlers', banished for their pacifism. It had taken all summer to cross the Caucasus and when they reached the allotted place, with nothing but their wagons for shelter, the ground was already covered in snow. The men were silent, the women wept. Larion Vassilevna Kalmykova had led the exodus from the Milky Waters; she started a psalm. When they had all finished there was just the sound of the wind. Larion said: 'We will winter here and in the spring we will move to a better place.'

But within a few weeks the winter had killed Larion Vassi-levna. Others perished too before the spring arrived. They never did move on. Over the years their adopted land became known to them as the Second Siberia.

I walked beside the cabins. They stuck out like ribs from the spine of the main road. Bow-legged men busied themselves in the yards. Women knelt in potato patches. A nostalgia hung over everything in Goryelovka, over its mud-walled barns and cherry trees, the tightly-scarved faces of the women, the pushed-up caps of the men. It was a nostalgia for the green land beyond the Caucasus, a nostalgia for the north, and I felt

it with them, standing before the pale-blue Orphan House and
its whitewashed picket fence.

One night, a generation or so after their arrival in Georgia, a
Doukhobor boy watched a star fall out of the sky and land on
one of his neighbours' houses. In the morning he noticed that
the people of that house had a brand-new baby. At the time
he was too terrified to mention the star to anyone, but years
later he began to hear others say what he'd always suspected:
that the baby born that night had come straight from Heaven
and was going to judge the universe.

The child was the fifth son of Vasily Verigin, and they named
him Pyotr.

In death, Pyotr Verigin dominates and divides the Doukhobors just as he did in life. His picture still hangs in the sacred
corner of dozens of homes – in Canada and Georgia and on
the Salsk steppe. In others his name is taboo.

It was through the Orphan House that Pyotr Verigin first
rose to power. With a hoard of about half a million roubles on
the premises, the Orphan House had developed some clout in
the community. When Verigin took over its running he began
to warn the Doukhobors that the Second Coming was almost
upon them. He himself started to behave in a mysterious way,
urging his followers to perform symbolic acts such as walking
around with their coats on inside out. He began to speak in
riddles and parables. Often it was not at all clear what he meant.
But, mused the Doukhobors, neither had people understood
Christ the first time around.

A man like Verigin was bound to split the Doukhobors, and
soon in Goryelovka there emerged two factions – the Large
Party and the Small Party. The Small Party said that control of
the Orphan House was their entitlement. The Large Party, who
were Verigin's supporters, said the same, and because they were

larger it was the Large Party that won the day. At a commemorative meeting of the Orphan House, while members of the Large
Party thronged around Verigin, the Small Party went off to tell
the authorities that this was the man who had acquired common
property for his own use, and who was also claiming to be
Christ and that wasn't right. He was duly arrested.

Verigin was sent to Archangel in the far north of Russia. For
five years he retained his authority with the Large Party through
letters and the visits of his disciples. At first he told them to
take control of the Orphan House by force; in Goryelovka,
troops were sent in to resist them.

Verigin kept up a stream of instructions to his followers.
They must, he said, 'pray to God with awe and expect at every
moment the coming of Verigin and the time when he will
clear all the Doukhobors and separate the believers from the
unbelievers'. His brother-in-law came to see him in the north
and returned to the Doukhobors with instructions: it was a
good thing to pray through the night because at dawn the Lord
was at his most free with his favours. For some time afterwards
the moonlit grass of the plains was filled with the praying figures
of the Large Party.

Verigin's five-year term expired. The courts casually gave him
another five years and transferred him to Siberia. There he came
across the works of Tolstoy and stepped up the strength of his
missives. He told the Doukhobors they must desist from drinking and smoking, must avoid eating meat and must remain
chaste. The chastity caused some debate back in Georgia and
split the Large Party into 'the Fleshers' and 'the Fasters'. Then
the command came that they must renounce all worldly goods,
free their cattle and live off only plants and water. Verigin, they
were told, was 'trying to eat the moss on which the reindeer is
feeding and he found it tasty'. They must also shed their clothes
and live naked like Adam and Eve.

But all this was benign compared to the order Verigin issued in 1895: the true Doukhobor must resist all attempts at conscription into the army.

At about the same time in Goryelovka, the Doukhobors received the order to supply the military with one man per household. So, heeding Verigin's advice, on the night of 28 June 1895 the Fleshers of the Large Party gathered all their weapons together and made a pile of them in the mountains. While they sang their psalms, the flames grew higher and sent a cascade of sparks into the night sky; the stocks of the guns burned, the barrels buckled. The Doukhobors stayed there until after the sun rose. Then they saw a group of Cossacks galloping across the plain towards them. The Cossacks encircled them, beat them with knouts and drove them into the local town. Two of the Doukhobors died in the assault.

After the burning of the guns, the Doukhobors were scattered again and a group was sent to Siberia under armed guard. The journey took the best part of a year. They were shown a hut at the mouth of the river Notora and their escort left them for the winter. They were 160 miles from the nearest village. Unsuitably clad for the cold, they slept in turns, half of them walking around the hut to keep warm while those sleeping wore the bulk of the clothes.

It was clear to more and more of the Doukhobors that their beliefs were irreconcilable with life under the tsar. They began to talk of emigration; Canada was mentioned. From Georgia a Doukhobor of the Large Party, named Pozdnayakov, was elected to go and seek Verigin's counsel. It was a hazardous journey as by now Verigin was prohibited from contacting his followers. He'd also had yet another five years added to his Siberian sentence. Travelling on a false passport, Pozdnayakov tracked down his leader. They met in secret and discussed the Canadian venture, and agreed its merits.

But Pozdnayakov was not impressed by Verigin. He found him 'vain and selfish' and far removed from the sufferings of his people. En route back to the Caucasus, Pozdnayakov called in on Tolstoy. He was not too impressed by the count either, but conceded that 'he seemed himself to be quite sincere and trying to do his best'.

After the 1905 revolution the Siberian Doukhobors were freed. They joined those in Canada who had already left Georgia. Pozdnayakov was among them, but by now he was severely opposed to Verigin. In the end he settled in California. His health broken by the Siberian years, he died there in 1921.

Pyotr Verigin himself died on a train in Canada in 1924, victim of an unexplained bomb attack.

The houses of Goryelovka had all either collapsed or were too big for the families that remained. The Doukhobors had been leaving the village ever since they'd first arrived here. I stayed with Luda and her extended family of six in a house that had once held twenty.

Luda was a tough woman with silver front teeth and a determination to keep going what remained of the kolkhoz. Once a week the Russian border guards came down from the hills and she sold them cheese. Last winter had been very bad. In October the Doukhobors lost the phones and electricity and, with the roads snow-clogged, remained in complete isolation for five months. In the barns were thirty tons of wool. Luda had heard of some Doukhobor wool merchants in Sochi and battled away to get transport and fuel. It took two months and many bribes to cross the mountains. She reached Sochi shortly after a consignment of Turkish wool had wrecked the market. The price she got didn't even cover the fuel. It was July now, and the winter was not far away; up here the winter is never far away.

Yet she herself was free from doubts. 'We'll survive. We always have.'

From Goryelovka, a mud track led out across the plains. Luda stood by her fence and pointed up the path: 'The place of the guns – carry on past the lake.'

The sun was bright on the far hills. They were green and even and broken only occasionally by a thin outcropping of rock. The Doukhobors knew these hills as the Sacred Heights, and on certain days used to dress up in their finest clothes and sing psalms as they filed up to the summit. No one I spoke to could remember when the practice ended or why.

The lake did not appear until I was practically upon it. Terns darted around its rim and beyond it was a narrow ravine. Built into the rock was a rough stone grotto, painted white. It was here that the Doukhobors gathered in 1895 and burned their guns.

An elderly man came sauntering out of the plain. A strand of grass hung from his mouth. He wore a corduroy cap and had for many years been a schoolteacher. Even before the burning of the guns, he said, this place had been a chosen site for the Doukhobors. The first settlers had planted a birch copse here when they arrived.

'In trees lives the soul of the land,' the old man said. 'For England it is the oak; for Japan the cherry. But for us Russians it is the birch.'

He had never known Russia; he had done his military service in Armenia. As a Doukhobor he used to love coming to this place, with its stream and its grotto and the sound of the wind in the birch leaves. But the previous year the border guards had cut down the last of the birch trees for firewood.

Above us the clouds stood unmoving in a milky blue sky.

'In other places people don't believe as we do.' He looked out across the plains – the harsh plains, the flower-filled plains, the plains of nine-month snows: 'But after belief, what is there left?'

The last evening in Gorelovka I went to see a man named Volodya Vladimirovich. He lived with his brother and his brother's wife. Volodya's nephew was standing on the roof, scything the grass that grew there. Volodya found it hard to turn his head. When I entered the room he twisted his whole upper body to greet me. Open on his desk was the twenty-fourth volume of Tolstoy's Collected Works. 'Holy Spirit,' I read over his shoulder, '... where there is love ...' A cool wind blew through the window.

In 1931, Volodya had been arrested. Ten years of jails and gulags followed. He had known cells so full of people he survived only by sucking at the keyhole for air. Now he was stooped in his high-backed chair. He said: 'I was always the lucky one. My health stood up.'

The sunlight deepened and filled the room with its orange glow. Volodya pulled from a drawer a pile of photographs and took one out. I'd seen this picture before. It had hung on the wall of a Doukhobor's house near Salsk. It was the picture of the interior of a sunlit forest, with summer leaves and the slender boles of Russian poplars. Beneath them lay a grassy mound, unadorned and unmarked.

Overleaf it read: 'Leo Tolstoy's grave. In the forest "Old Reservation" there rises a modest, right-angled hillock. Stefan Zweig says: "This is the most beautiful, most impressive, most touching grave in the world."'

Volodya pressed the picture upon me. It has remained with me and has sat on my desk ever since.

The kolkhoz mechanic had to drive into town. I waited for him beside the road for the first leg of the journey north, back into

Russia. It was dawn. Rain was spitting at the dust. Over the roofs of the houses, over the storks' nests, lightning flashed around the peaks; briefly the sun broke through the underside of the cloud, but in that morning air lurked the first chill of winter.